IMPORTANT:
PLEASE READ CAREFULLY REGARDING THE
DOWNLOADING OF THE AUDIO RECORDINGS
WHICH ARE ESSENTIAL TO RECEIVING THE
MAXIMUM BENEFIT FROM THIS BOOK

In order to achieve the maximum from the book, it will be essential for you download and listen to the *2 Audio Recordings* that are an integral part of the entire book experience. These Audio Recordings can be downloaded from the following website:

http://qltseminars.com/LivingLifebyChoiceDownloads.aspx

It is highly recommended that the audio recordings are downloaded prior to you beginning to read the book.

In addition, all of charts and graphs found within the book can also be downloaded from the same website.

If you have any difficulty in your attempts to download the Audio Recordings face feel free to contact me directly.

tmahas@qltseminars.com

Best regards,

Tom Mahas & Elena Sotomayor

LIVING LIFE
BY CHOICE ...
NOT CHANCE

The Tools and Techniques to Take Control of Your Life

With

2 Self-Hypnosis Audio Recordings
Specially Designed to Ensure Your Success

TOM MAHAS BA, MA AND
ELENA SOTOMAYOR CHC

BALBOA.
PRESS
A DIVISION OF HAY HOUSE

Cover design by Rhett Nacson

E-mail:
Tom Mahas: tmahas@qltseminars.com
Elena Sotomayor: contacto@qualitylifetraining.com

Balboa Press books may be ordered through booksellers or by contacting:

Balboa Press
A Division of Hay House
1663 Liberty Drive
Bloomington, IN 47403
www.balboapress.com.au
1-(877) 407-4847

Every attempt has been made to identify and contact owners of copyright for permission to reproduce material in this book. However any copyright holders who have been inadvertently omitted from acknowledgments and credits should contact the author. Any omissions will be rectified in subsequent editions.

The author of this book does not dispense medical advice or prescribe the use of any technique as a form of treatment for physical, emotional, or medical problems without the advice of a physician, either directly or indirectly. The intent of the author is only to offer information of a general nature to help you in your quest for emotional and spiritual well-being. In the event you use any of the information in this book for yourself, which is your constitutional right, the author and the publisher assume no responsibility for your actions.

Printed in the United States of America

ISBN: 978-1-4525-0236-6 (sc)
ISBN: 978-1-4525-0237-3 (e)

Balboa Press rev. date: 10/07/2011

DEDICATION

I dedicate this book to my daughters, Maria and Fernanda, whose love and support allowed me to pursue my dreams.

Elena

I dedicate this book to Leon Nacson who has provided endless support and encouragement in so many ways – for so many years. In addition, I am dedicating this book to each person who has ever attended my Seminars – because, perhaps without any of them knowing it, each became '*my teacher*'.

Tom

ACKNOWLEDGEMENT

We would also like to express our appreciation to Carol Shalek-Saarela for her hours of work in proof-reading this manuscript. Her time, work and effort are so greatly appreciated.

Lastly, a special mention needs to be made of a software program, Dragon NaturallySpeaking (a voice recognition software program from Nuance Communications, Inc.). This entire book (except for its charts & graphs), has been dictated, rather than needing to be typed by using this software … so many thanks to Nuance for their brilliant software program.

CONTENTS

PART 1

PREFACE

By Tom Mahas

In 2003 I had a stroke. That stroke, for all practical purposes, had for a period of time severed my mind from my body. Immediately from the time I was in the ER to a few days after, nearly all my thoughts remained just thoughts, impotent thoughts. Even the most elementary thought had no consequences. A thought to move my hand, let alone just one of my fingers, was futile. So was the thought to reach out and touch the hand of my wife standing near my bed. It was the most horrible, devastating and the most frightening experience I ever had. I couldn't even move the muscles in my face to smile. It was as if I had been "buried alive." The strangest, perhaps the worst part of that experience was that unlike being in a coma, where one is not in full contact with the outside world. I could see, hear and feel everything around me but I couldn't respond back. What I did feel was extreme panic and fear. It was not the fear of dying though, it was the fear of not dying and yet having to remain the way I was, forever. I remember praying, *"Please let me die, rather than remain this way with only impotent thoughts.'*

Obviously, as I now understand, that prayer was, in fact, an affirmation of my desire to regain the life of quality I once knew and took for granted. This desire was so intense, and corning from the very essence of my being, that I actually could sense that some significant shift or realignment within me was taking place. And to this clay, the

1

most adequate way I can describe what took place is to say '*I chose to fight*'. I chose to fight back, and shatter the coffin I found myself in. I chose to return to the land of the living!" It was, I believe, the power of my *inner anger* and *rage*, that gave me the strength to fight back and claim what I felt was rightfully mine – and that was to once again *live a life of quality* rather than *just living*.

Looking back, I am still amazed at how quickly my situation turned around. Within only a few hours my arm, which I was unable to move, could be lifted slightly and after a day I was able to reach out and not only touch an object but to actually lightly grip and hold it. Step-by-step, movement by movement I slowly regained my coordination, as well as my strength. I once again was able to form words and make those words understood by others. With the help of the hospital speech therapists and physical therapists, things quickly returned to some level of normalcy. I could see improvement sometimes the matter of a mere few hours. Not only could I now hold the fork, I could actually put food on it and reach my mouth with it. Strength was returning to my legs and I was able to leave the bed and walk. I also was able, admittedly somewhat slurred, to again talk and communicate freely. At the time, my recovery seemed to be a long, tedious, demanding and never ending experience. However, from a more objective perspective, it was a mere six days later that I actually was able to walk out of that hospital, with only a cane to support me. *In six days, my world was re-created. On the seventh, I rested.*

I must stop here and put things in somewhat better perspective. The hospital care and therapy I received had been excellent and in no way am I attempting to minimize the impact that the doctors, nurses and therapists had on my recovery. I had a lot of people supporting me in my recovery, but most of all it was the support I received from Elena that gave me desire to fight back in the first place. I'm grateful to each and every one of them for the help and support they provided. But I've learned first-hand that even the best medical care cannot '*force*' any human body to heal. As every medical practitioner knows from experience, the magic of medicine is profound but if the patient gives up the will to live or to even improve, there is nothing medical science or anyone can do about it. When a human being gives up the '*will/ desire*' to '*live*' the game is over. And in turn, when a person *refuses to give up* the desire to live - expect miracles. The most damaged and physically broken have been known to do their own *"Lazarus Routine"* and rejoined the living, totally whole and totally healed.

... and so the purpose of this book.

Elena and I have taught thousands of people over 30 years about the power of the mind and we truly *believe* everything is possible if we learn to use the power of our minds correctly. It was my *belief* that I could fight back and regain a life of quality I so desperately sought, that allowed me to do so. However, in no way did my 30 years of teaching about the mind make me any more capable than you or anyone else of using my mind to change my reality. It is the *power of belief* that provides the mind its power. Reread that statement a thousand times if you must but understand what we are trying to say. Your power, your real power to be who you really are, have what you really want and to make things happen in your life, lies in you learning to release the power of your *Mind* and use it to *its full potential*.

Tom and Elena

Quality Life Training

INTRODUCTION:

This *User's Guide for the Mind* and the MP3 Recordings are meant to provide you not only a clear and straight forward understanding of how your *Mind* works but more importantly, provide you the actual tools and techniques to tap its nearly unlimited potential so that you can achieve a life that you desire. That is, a **Life of Quality**, which of course would mean: good health, rewarding relationships, wealth & prosperity.

But why the *Mind?* That's simple -- it is your *Mind* that determines **1)** how you see & perceive the world, **2)** how you choose to do what you do, **3)** how you act/react to what happens or doesn't happen to you and **4)** how you can get what you want (your *plan of action* and the *strategies* you use to get what you want).

Yet, regardless of the importance of your *Mind*, chances are you have never been taught how your *Mind* works, how to control it, let alone how to tap its full potential. Learning to use and control the *Mind* is definitely not on the list of "*what every person should know in order for them to achieve the quality life they are entitled to.*" Yet without such understanding, achieving a **Life of Quality** will be most probably **by chance** ... rather than **by choice**. And that just isn't good enough. It's your *Mind* and you have the right to know how to tap its full potential and use it to its maximum. It's like giving someone a Porsche, without giving them the keys to drive it.

Most likely there have been numerous aspects of your life that you have wanted to improve, whether it was your health, your financial situation, your relationships, etc. but you had no idea how to do it. In addition, you probably have had a few *'unwanted habits'* or *'ways of behaving'* (i.e. over-eating, smoking, nail biting, quick to anger -- to name just a few) that you truly wanted to change but couldn't, regardless of your *"determination"* and *"willpower"*. It seems sometimes that regardless of how you put *"your Mind to something"* nothing ever seems to really improve and sometime, things even seem to get worse.

Unfortunately, such *"failure"* can leave you with little option but to conclude that 1) you were simply too weak and powerless to make any significant changes in your life and/or 2) you'll never really be able to change aspects of your life that really need to be changed, as obviously you were born a certain way and must remain that way.

The truth is, your so-called *"failure or inability to change"* was most likely due to a lack of understanding as to how your *Mind* actually works, rather than to any weakness or powerlessness on your part. If you would have been taught how to tap into your *Subconscious Level,*(where by the way, habits and patterns are in fact located), you would have been able to have eliminated those undesired *Habits* and *Behavioral Patterns* from your life quickly and easily.

Unfortunately, no one taught you how to do that and that's just not good enough, is it? It's your *Mind* and as you are being held responsible for its activities, you have the right to know how it works so that you could make it work for you rather than against you. And that's precisely what you're about to learn how to do ... so read on.

But First, A Few Requirements ...

The following are the minimum requirements necessary to receive the maximum benefit from this *User's Guide:*

1. Have the willingness/desire *to improve* the *Quality of Your Life*: whether it be in regards to your health, relationships, wealth and/or spiritually,

2. Have the willingness *to change*: whether it is changing your thinking, changing your beliefs about yourself and the world you live in and/or changing your behavior and the way you are do things.

3. Have the willingness to take responsibility for your life and the choices you make -- thereby becoming a *Master* of your life rather than being victimized by it.

In regards to the book itself, we have done our best to keep this *User's Guide* as simple and readable as we could without compromising any of the essential information that we know you will need to achieve the life you desire. We are asking of you to do the same ... keep it simple -- because it is simple! Don't approach what you are about to read with the belief or attitude that *"learning to take control of your life"* needs to be difficult or complicated, because it doesn't! If you can read about it, you will be able to easily master it as well. On the other hand, don't fall into the trap of believing that just because something is 'simple', it couldn't possibly be of much value. Think about it, *"Everything is actually simple when you learn how to it."* Take for example, professional Figure Skaters -- it's because they have mastered the *'Art of Skating'* that they make skating look so very, very easy and simple. Just try it and you'll discover very quickly just how easy and simple it is ... that is, if you don't break a few bones in the process. In the same way, after you learn to *Master Your Mind,* you will make 'achieving *success'* look so very, very easy and simple to others. Because it will be, for you!

Lastly, we are asking you not to just skim through the book and focus on only those topics that seem relevant or of interest to you. As you could imagine, it just wouldn't be possible to have included every possible type of problem in any one book. Fortunately, there was really no need for us to have tried to do so. Once you *learn how* to *program* your *Subconscious* for a *'New Job',* you can easily program for a *'New Car'* or anything else you desire in your life. It's because the principles and procedures for achieving *'Success'* remain the same regardless what you are programming for.

PLEASE NOTE

As you will need to listen to these Audio Recordings for 21 days, you may wish to do so at work or other times when you are not at your computer. we would suggest '*downloading*' "*The Relaxation Training Exercise*" and "*Embedding Techniques*" audio files to your MP3, iPod, or other audio devices.

. . . So with that,

let's begin creating the life

of quality that you not only

desire but so rightly deserve.

THE MIND

**You can have and be anything
you want . . . well kind of!**

We won't apologize for seemingly putting limitations on what you can have and what you can do -- we would have to apologize, if *we* didn't. We, as human beings, are part of this Universe and therefore must abide by the laws that govern everything in it. As we are not birds; we cannot fly by merely flapping our arms nor are *we* redwood trees; so we will never be able to grow roots and grow to the height of 100 feet. We are not trying to be silly or facetious by using these as examples. It is just that so often, especially in the area of personal growth & development, we are told, by numerous authors and seminar presenters, that we can do, have and be *anything we want* -- if only we put our *Minds to it.*

We are assuming that these authors and seminar presenters, if they were asked, would agree that there are, of course, *"some limitations"* as to what we can actually do, be and have. Many however, rather than acknowledging these limitations, tend to continue to make these sweeping statements regarding our *"unlimited potential."* We say this comfortably, as both of us have most probably made similar sweeping *'statements of fact'* in our own seminars in the past. They were never said to lie or deceive but rather to capture the imagination and motivate those, who we wanted to believe, were hanging on our every word.

13

Even if such sweeping statements were made, we're not suggesting that we believe anyone has ever left our various seminars believing that they could actually fly if they really, really wanted to, by flapping their arms. But looking back, perhaps we could have been of greater service to our students by spending more time explaining that our *Minds* are truly *'unlimited'* but only within 'the limits of this Universe' that we live in ... and more importantly, so what if our *Minds* have some limits! Even though we may not be able to fly by flapping our arms, doesn't mean we can't somehow fly. Does it? We just might need to use our *Mind's* unlimited *"Creative Ability"* to dream-up an airplane to help us do it, as the Wright Brothers did. Simply said, we are *unlimited as* to *what* we *can have and do.* However though; we may be somewhat *limited as* to *how* we *can achieve it,* but achieve it we can. We just might need to be very *'Creative'* as to how we will do it.

Having said that, let's begin to look at your *Mind* and the power it has to create for you the life you desire.

Tapping the Power of the *Mind:*

The real *'power'* of the *Mind* lies in the *'desires'* it has and the *'beliefs'* it holds true. Therefore, if you want something, and we mean really, really, really want something ... you must 1) desire it passionately and 2) believe without any doubt that you will have it. It is only with such *'real desire'* and *'unwavering belief'* that you will be able to release the full power of your *Mind.* And it is with this winning formula ... that whatever you asked for, can be yours.

To better understand why the power of desire and belief is the key to unlocking your *Mind* and its great potential, we need to step back and get a better understanding of the *Mind* itself. Perhaps we should begin by asking:

- How does one even define the *Mind?*

- How does one separate the *Mind* from the brain?

- How does one separate the Mind/brain from the body?

The problem in attempting to answer these questions requires that we artificially attempt to separate the most incredible, integrated and complex *'living system'* on this planet, the human being. Impressed? You should be!

However, let's stop and ask a very important question about this amazing *"Multitasking Life-Support System"*: Who is controlling it? Who (or what) is controlling the controls of your Controller? (Is this a tongue twister or a Mind twister?) Simply stated: Who is controlling your *Mind*? Are you really? Oh, you might own it and have possession of it - but ARE YOU REALLY, REALLY CONTROLLING IT? Most probably not - and if not, why not? It's yours and nobody else's. Besides, you are being held responsible for everything it does and does not do. If it makes a mistake or it makes the wrong choice, if it doesn't learn fast enough, or well enough, if it doesn't achieve enough or succeeds enough -- the world judges and blames you. Does it not?

Worst yet, you most probably judge and blame yourself for all of your *Mind's* faults, failures and limitations. If it finds itself having difficulty in loving and being loved, difficulty in giving or receiving, too slow to react or even too quick, it will be you and not your *Mind* that will be judged for being unloving and too self-centered, for being oversensitive or even insensitive to others, etc. And just perhaps, they're right. For has it not been said that *"You are what you think you are."*

Could it not be possible that what you think *'you are'* is simply what your *Mind* *"thinks"* you are -and everything else, your brain and body, are merely the container you have to house the *Mind*, to give it a place to reside. And by residing in the body/brain, the *Mind* is no longer just limited to having thoughts, it now has the ability and the means by which it can manifest and give form to its/your thoughts.

It would follow that if you don't start controlling the controls of your Controller, the Controller will continue to control you and the *'quality of your life'* will remain at its mercy.

So if you could learn how to take charge and control your *Mind*, you would in fact be learning how to take charge and control your life, and ultimately, your destiny. That's right your destiny! If you believe you have *'Free Will'*, then it would have to follow that the quality of your happiness, health and prosperity has not, repeat, has not and could not have been predetermined or predestined. Rather, the quality of your life is being determined by you, through *your thoughts and actions, and only yours.*

Therefore, you must choose either to: **1)** leave the quality of your life to *chance* and hope for the best or **2)** *choose* to step in and take charge of your life and determine your own destiny. Once again, and never forget it, the choice is and always will be yours!

If your choice is to take charge of your life, then get comfortable, as we are going on a journey - a journey deep within the inner world of your *Mind.*

Understanding
the Mind and the Brain:

To gain a better understanding as to how the *Mind* works, we will view the *Mind* as having three levels or divisions:

1. *The Conscious Mind*
2. *The Subconscious Mind*
3. *The Unconscious Mind*

MIND CHART

BETA↑ 14 cps	Outer Physical World of the **CONSCIOUS MIND**	Logic & Reason Sight/Sound/Smell/Taste/Touch
ALPHA 7-10 cps	*UPPER* Inner Subjective World — *Being Centered* — **SUBCONSCIOUS MIND**	Daydreaming/Memory/Learning/ Behavior Patterns/Habits/Night Dreams/Imagination
THETA 4-7 cps	*LOWER*	Painless Dentistry /Surgery/ Natural Childbirth/etc.
DELTA 0-4 cps	**UNCONSCIOUS MIND**	Deep Sleep/Basic Survival Patterns Coma

*CPS= Cycles Per Second

About the Mind Chart:

This *'Mind Chart'* provides various types of information regarding the *Mind*. On the left side, in *Column 1*, information is provided regarding the *'Brain Frequencies'* that are associated with the three levels of the *Mind: Conscious, Subconscious* and *Unconscious*. These brain frequencies are measured in cycles per second (CPS) and are obtained when a person is being monitored by an *electroencephalograph*, often referred to simply as an *EEG monitor.*

An *EEG* can be used for a variety of purposes medically. Usually, it is used to monitor the brain for the purpose of determining how the brain is functioning or malfunctioning. The information that is obtained from an *EEG* will often play a vital role in determining if a person's brain is functioning properly, or if some problem exists. It is often used to determine whether or not a person is in a coma and/or is *'brain dead.'* Determining if a person is *'brain dead'* has become extremely important in deciding whether the *'life support system,'* that maybe keeping an individual *'alive'*, could be medically and ethically *"turned off."*

As you view the various ranges of brain frequencies (Beta, Alpha, Theta, Delta) it will become apparent that quite distinct *'mental abilities'* directly correspond to various brain frequencies. These *Mind abilities* are listed on the right-hand side of the chart.

BETA *(The Conscious Mind):*

When the brain is functioning in the *Beta range,* the brain frequencies would generally be 14 cps or higher. You will note that the chart indicates that when the brain is functioning at these higher frequencies, you would be considered *'Conscious'* - therefore it is referred to as the *'**Conscious Mind.'*** When functioning at this *Beta Level,* you would be capable of interacting with the *'The Physical/Outside World'* -- via your five senses of sight - sound – taste - smell - touch. In addition, when you would be functioning at this *Beta Level,* you would have access to your abilities to use *Logic and Reason*, as well as, have the ability to communicate via *language*. It is said that as an adult, you would be spending close to 85% of your *'awake state'* in this *Beta range.*

ALPHA/THETA *(The Subconscious Mind)*:

These levels it is generally felt to be where the *'Subconscious Mind'* resides and with it, your long-term memory, your learning ability, Behavior Patterns, Habits and Imagination, as well as, where most of your nighttime and daytime dreaming (daydreaming) takes place. Therefore, the *Subconscious Mind* is the keeper and guardian of your Behavioral Patterns, Habits and Beliefs. As a result, Behavioral Patterns, Habits and Beliefs are below normal Conscious awareness and special training is usually required to access them.

If we can draw an analogy, the *Subconscious* functions very much like the internal memory of a computer. This internal memory controls and determines what the computer can and cannot do. In the same way, the programs and beliefs found within your *Subconscious* determine what you can and cannot do. Change, modify or update these programs and beliefs and suddenly your bio-computer *(the Mind/body)* has had its abilities and potential modified and updated as well. Simple, isn't it?

Be assured we will go into this in much greater detail in the next chapter. For now, just be aware that it is your *Subconscious Mind* that you will need to focus on if you are to bring about any significant changes in your life. The brain frequencies generally associated with the **Alpha Level** is between 7 and 14 cps.

DELTA (The Unconscious *Mind)*:

If you break the word down, it's easy to understand the workings of the **Unconscious Mind**: **Un** = *'not'* or *'without'* and **Conscious** = *'awareness'*. Of the three levels, the *Unconscious Mind* remains perhaps, the least known and the most mysterious level of your Mind. The reason for this is that most people have little or no awareness when they are functioning at this level. Therefore, it has been extremely difficult to receive any reliable feedback about the going-ons within the *Unconscious*.

What is known about the *Unconscious Mind* is that it plays a vital role in maintaining and controlling the most basic of your survival programs. Survival programs such as: breathing, circulation, heart rate, etc. What we do know is that we drift into the upper levels of the *Unconscious* during our deep sleep. It's interesting to note that people who are in a coma, are for the most part, functioning exclusively in this *Unconscious Realm*. The brain frequencies generally accepted as representing the *Unconscious Mind* are from 0.5-4 cps. You might be interested to know that if the brain frequency recorded is '0' cps', that individual would be considered *"brain-dead."*

UNDERSTANDING YOUR SUBCONSCIOUS:

As you will note within the *Mind Chart*, the *Subconscious Level makes* reference to *'Being Centered'*. This is a term that we will use to indicate an ideal state where you are and will remain <u>*'Consciously Aware'*</u> of your *Subconscious Realm* which normally is *'below your conscious awareness'* (**Sub** = *below* and **Conscious** = *awareness*). However, through your training that you will receive by listening to the enclosed Audio Recordings, you will learn to not only enter your *Subconscious* at will but be totally conscious and aware while doing so in order to create, modify or eliminate any **Behavioral Patterns** or **Habits** you desire.

Being Centered:

To achieve this ideal state of *'Being Centered'*, you will need to be both physically and mentally relaxed and remain in a relaxed state. Of course, *'Being Centered'* will be a relative term in regards to actual brain frequencies. One can actually be *'Centered'* even though one is functioning at the upper realms of the Alpha Level or the lower realms of the Theta Level. Therefore, *'Being Centered,* as we are using the term throughout this book, is not attempting to indicate any specific brain frequency but rather it is meant to indicate your *Mind* is functioning somewhere within your *'Subconscious Realm.'*   Having said this, whenever you are required to *'Center'* yourself, simply ensure that you are sufficiently relaxed both physically and mentally. When you are, you will naturally be functioning within your *Subconscious Realm*.

The Need to Master Mind Shifting
by Listening to the *Relaxation Training Exercise*:

Normally during your awake state, you will be functioning primarily at the *Beta Level* where you are both physically and mentally interacting with the physical world, whether communicating with people, driving in traffic, writing reports, etc. Therefore, unless the stimuli from the outside world can be significantly minimized and/or eliminated, it tends to become extremely difficult, if not nearly impossible, to shift from the *Conscious Level* to the hush and quiet world of the *Subconscious*. However, you can learn to easily make this shift whenever you desire by listening to the *Relaxation Training*. It has been designed to help you learn how to *'tune-out'* the outside stimuli and interference of your *Conscious level* at will and shift easily into the realm of your *Subconscious*.

By the way, mastering this ability to shift your awareness will be easily learned and mastered. When we say it is *easy,* we mean it. We can say this because you are already able to enter your *Subconscious Mind* and you do so regularly. Whenever you relax your thinking, such as when you daydream or attempt to recall information from the past, you are in fact entering and functioning at the upper levels of your *Subconscious*. If your mind wanders, even for a few moments while reading this book, you are most probably slipping into the upper realms of your *Subconscious*. In addition, you pass through your *Subconscious* every night on your way to sleep, as well as numerous times throughout the night when your *Mind* is dreaming. We told you it was easy, so don't even think for one moment that you might not be able to do it. If you can sleep or daydream—you can easily enter your *Subconscious*.

Programming the Subconscious:

When information is received by the *Subconscious,* it is 'stored' or 'embedded' physically in the brain as a neurological pattern or pathway (see the brain chart below). In fact, all information that we retain and remember is embedded in the cells of the brain by a chemical/electrical process. The cells that have the information embedded become bonded and form a pattern and this new pattern is referred to as a neurological (brain) *pattern* or *pathway*. Whenever a *pattern* or *pathway* is activated, the information embedded becomes available to the brain/mind system. These *patterns* or *pathways* can store a variety of different types of information. The *'information'* that a *pattern* or *pathway* can have embedded can be:

1. Factual material such as: 'that person's name is ...'to 'the lyrics of an entire song' or as complex as:

2. The behavioral actions of actually 'playing the entire song on the piano from memory'.

But even more importantly, these *patterns* or *pathways* can contain a complex *behavioral response (with includes a strong emotional response)* that can be activated by some *stimulus* that has taken place in the *outside world,* An example might be when you are crossing the street and you notice a speeding car headed towards you (the *stimulus*) and you immediately jump out of its way (your *response*). In this type of case, it is an *'automatic* response' which is known as simply *'a habit.'* It has been said that 99% of our human behavior is in fact *behavioral responses* or *habits.*

Brain Pathways/Patterns

Whatever we learn is recorded in the brain as a *Pathway* or *Pattern.* These *Pathways* or *Patterns* can contain *information* as simple as *'A Person's Name'* or as complex as *'Remembering the Lyrics to an entire Song'. 'A Desire, Need* or *'The person's face'* can become the __STIMULUS__*'* that will cause the *Pathway or Pattern* which contains the *'desired information',* to __RESPOND__ by making the *information* it contains available.

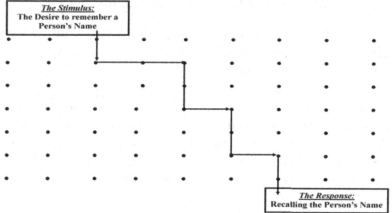

As you can imagine, you would have literally thousands of such *patterns* or *pathways* embedded in your brain. And whether they were *factual material patterns* or *behavioral response patterns* your *mind* would consider them '*factual* or 'true.' This fact is essential for us to understand-

1. Why it is so difficult to *"change our minds"* and

2. Why we can become upset when conflicting information attempts to embed itself as *"also* true."

Let us look at a few examples: Let's say you have a factual pattern that states "*His name is Robert*" but during a conversation with someone, that person says '*His name is George.*' Chances are you will find that you (or at least your mind) will go through moments of mild confusion and momentarily goes blank because the information you just received is in 'conflict' with your own factual pattern that knows (or believes) that his name is Robert. Perhaps you will say *"Who?"* or *"Oh, I thought his name was Robert."* And until you are able to resolve this conflict, you will continue to feel somewhat uneasy until this conflict is reconciled, either by you discovering you had the wrong name associated with the person or the other person did.

Of course this is a relatively insignificant conflict and it has only been used to help you understand *"how the Subconscious reacts to having its patterns challenged"*. Regardless of how insignificant this example might actually be, to your *Subconscious*, it is very significant as it hates having one of its patterns or pathways challenged. Simply said, your *Subconscious*, by its nature, resists change. This is not a flaw; it's a valuable characteristic of how your *Subconscious* functions,

If your *Subconscious* would change its patterns or pathways frivolously, the security and reliability that you have come to expect from your Subconscious would be greatly compromised. As an example, when you are driving your car and the light changes from green to red, you simply expect your foot to hit the brake without having to consciously tell your foot to do so. If this wasn't the case, every time the light changes from green to red, you would have to decide what your response will be. Chances are that, by the time you did this, you would have already entered the intersection. So yes, we have come to depend upon our *Subconscious* to do its job of reacting flawlessly and automatically when it needs to.

Just A Thought: If you do expect this flawless behavior from your *Subconscious* then don't mess with it by feeding it alcohol/drugs and denying it sleep which will prevent it from doing its job properly ... besides, such messing around can kill you.

If the *Subconscious* Resists Change... Can It Be Changed?

The fact that your *Subconscious* resists change, can present a significant problem for you if you desire to change, modify or deactivate some *pattern* that may be preventing you from achieving a better quality life. Therefore, it becomes necessary for us to discuss what can be done to change, modify or deactivate undesirable *patterns* when required.

It's important to understand that when you *"deactivate" patterns* in your *Subconscious,* you are not actually deleting or erasing it from the *Subconscious.* If you were to attempt to physically remove a *brain pattern*, it would require you to take some very drastic action, such as, **1)** surgically removing the actual brain cells which make up that *pattern* or **2)** applying an electrical shock to the brain in order to 'scramble' the area of the brain that contains the undesired *pattern.*

We are not trying to be flippant when we say this. Applying electric shocks to the brain in order to scramble neurological patterns is an actual medical procedure referred to as **Electric Shock Treatment** or more accurately **Electroconvulsive Therapy (ECT).** ECT is a psychiatric treatment in which seizures are electrically induced in anesthetized patients for various therapeutic effects.

As drastic as these options might be, anything short of actually surgically removing or electrically scrambling the *pattern,* does not provide any guarantee that the *pattern* could not resurface and reactivate at some later date. Once a *pattern* is embedded ... it is yours forever. So embed beliefs and habits with caution! This is really powerful stuff, isn't it? If knowing this doesn't 'shock' you into watching your thoughts and listening to what you say to and about yourself, we're not sure what will.

But Wait! There is a Third Option ...

Besides *'Electric Shock Treatment'* or *'Surgical Removal'* to eliminate unwanted *'beliefs and habits'* there is a third option, one that you might prefer.

As you are now able to enter the realms of the *Subconscious,* you are now also able to directly *'deactivate'* any of your *"unwanted belief habit/patterns'* by embedding a new *pattern* of your choice. With minimal reinforcement it will become your new, predominant *pattern.* Think about that! And think seriously! What this means is that if you experience any unwanted response/reaction to any situation, you will be able to change your response/reaction, if you desire. So if you are now finding yourself absolutely panic stricken when you are required to go to the dentist, you will be able to change your reaction from panic to remaining totally calm and relaxed. Now that's impressive, isn't it?

Embedding New Patterns in Your Subconscious

If you want something and there is a conflicting *pattern* which has already been embedded in the *Subconscious,* it can be extremely difficult (not impossible, just more difficult) to embed your new desired *pattern.* For example: you might already have a strong embedded *fear-pattern* of getting up and talking to a group of people. Now however, you desire to eliminate that fear so that you would be able *"to speak in front of people while remaining calm, relaxed and very articulate."* In this case, your new desired *behavioral-pattern* is in direct conflict with one which has already been embedded, namely the one that has you reacting with nervousness, tension and *"stage fright."* This conflict will need to be resolved if you ever hope to overcome your fear of public speaking.

To resolve this conflict you will need to go directly to your *Subconscious* and strongly implant and activate your new desired *behavioral-response* while deactivating the *fear-pattern* of talking in front of people. (*Remember, learning to go directly to your Subconscious and embed new patterns and/or replace the undesirable ones, is precisely what you're learning to do when you listen to the "Relaxation Training Exercise.")* Your newly embedded pattern would then need to be reinforced sufficiently to ensure that your *Subconscious* acknowledges it as the *predominant pattern* to use when you are confronted with public speaking.

However, just desiring a new *behavioral-response* will not create or replace your predominant *fear-pattern* if you continue to reinforce the old *pattern,* i.e. by continuing to affirm that *"you hate talking in front of people."* Remember, until your new *pattern* is firmly embedded and becomes your predominant one, the old *pattern* will remain active within your *Subconscious.*

Let's take some time to look at this very important process of deactivating & activating *'belief and habit patterns'* within the *Subconscious.* As an analogy, perhaps we could imagine a neurological pathway as a pathway down a hill rather than in the brain. Let's say, that when it rains (stimulus), the rain water (taking the path of least resistance) will naturally flow down the path/rut that has formed down the hillside by previous rain. Let's imagine further, that at the bottom of this hill is your house. Therefore, every time there is a heavy rain, water rushes down the path and floods your house. The question is: *"What can you do about it?"*

Actually, there will be a few options:

> **Option #1:** You could physically move the house so that it is no longer in direct line with the path of water flowing from the hill.

> **Option #2:** You could leave and find someplace else to live.

> **Option #3:** You could do nothing, except pray that it doesn't rain.

> **Option #4:** You could take a shovel and dig a new pathway from the top of the hill down to the bottom, in such a fashion, that when water ran down that pathway, it would bypass your house completely.

Embedding a New Brain Pattern

Whenever a '*New Brain Pattern*', is embedded, it will need to be reinforced in order to ensure that *1)* It becomes '*Activated*' as the '*New*' predominant pattern and that *2)* The '*Old Pattern*' is '*Deactivated*'. Remember, even though the '*Old Pattern*' becomes deactivated, it is not actually removed or eliminated and therefore, it can always be reactivated by *Stress* or some *Dramatic Experience* in the future.

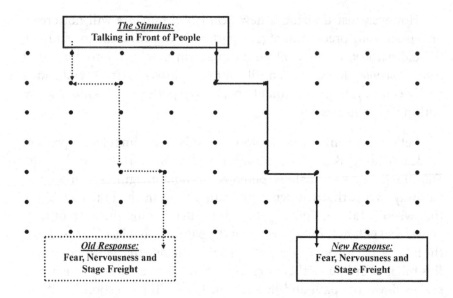

The most logical choice would be **Option #4,** isn't it? Yet an interesting thing about **Option #4,** is that after you dig the *new pathway (creating a new 'Belief/Habit')* that would bypass your house, you would also need to block the *old pathway* with rocks or by some other means *(deactivating the old pathway)* to ensure that in the future, any excessive water would flow down your new desired pathway *(activating the new pathway).*

And lastly, you would want to periodically reinforce the new pathway to ensure that it remains the *primary path* that the water will flow down in the future.

A Few More Things to Get the Results You Desire:

Embed your new *Affirmation/Desires* directly into the *Subconscious* rather than taking the longer and more indirect route via your *Conscious Mind*. To do this, *Relax and **Center*** yourself and begin repeating your *Affirmations* directly to your *Subconscious Level.*

Once the new *Belief-Pattern* has been embedded in your *Subconscious*, it will need to be reinforced for a short period of time thereafter. This is especially true if your *Subconscious* already has a conflicting *Pattern* embedded.

Once your new *Belief-Pattern* has been embedded in your *Subconscious*, you can reinforce it at any time you desire. You do not need to be at the *Subconscious Level* to do so. You can reinforce them while you are jogging, exercising, walking, doing any type of mundane work or when you are just sitting quietly taking a break.

A *Belief-Pattern* is a statement of *"truth"* for your *Subconscious*. Therefore, if for any reason the *old belief* surfaces, you must not, in any way, reinforce it and thereby re-empower it. You must consciously negate the undesired *Belief-Pattern* immediately, and do so each and every time it comes to *Mind*. A very simple but very effective way to negate any undesirable *Belief-Pattern*, is by simply saying *"**That's not true**"* as soon as it enters your Mind. By saying that *"That's not* true' you will be negating that *Belief-Pattern's* truthfulness and making it *powerless* within your *Subconscious*.

Also beware that an old, negative *Belief-Pattern* can resurface at any time. It might not be tomorrow or next week but it can resurface even years later if you to slip back into a *Mindset* of self-doubt. If this does happen, remember to not only negate the undesired pattern but to reinforce the desired pattern as well. It's important to remember that the old *Belief-Pattern* will always remain in your *Subconscious* ... forever. The most you can do is keep that *Undesired Pattern* deactivated.

Case in Point: All smokers know that *habit-patterns* can be easily reactivated if they have ever attempted to quit smoking. Once the habit of smoking is embedded, smokers remain vulnerable to start smoking again at any time in the future. It doesn't matter if they haven't smoked in 30 years. Stress or some traumatic experience can, and often does, reactivate their long, lost desire to smoke. The same can be said for over eating, drug addictions, etc. We simply never forget. ***And never forget that!***

Isn't it also true that once you've learned to ride a bike, that learning *pattern* is never forgotten? Even after 30 years of never having ridden a bike, that learned *pattern* can resurface after only a few minutes and you will be riding a bike as well as you did 30 years ago. Amazing, isn't it?!

Hopefully you now appreciate why it's so very, very important to prevent children from ever developing undesirable habits, whether it be smoking, using drugs, over eating, abusing and/or bullying others, etc. These *patterns* of behavior will become embedded in their little *Subconscious Minds* ... **Forever!**

The Need to Listen to "*The Relaxation Training Exercise*"

We know you are eager to get on with the real *'meat'* of various techniques being offered in this book and we assure you that we understand your eagerness. We both however, have seen the consequences of those who tried to *"skip ahead'* by not listening to *"The Relaxation Training Exercise"* for the full *21 days*. In most cases, they reported back that perhaps they did receive some good results initially, but after a few weeks, their results waned and the benefits they received from the various techniques began to significantly slip from what they had initially achieved.

This is not meant to be heavy-handed but rather it is meant to emphasize a very important point, and that is, (excuse the cliché) *"haste makes waste."* Generally speaking, it takes about 21 days (3 weeks) to realign and take charge of the *Subconscious Mind*. Therefore, to guarantee that the realignment of your *Subconscious* remains permanent, we urge you to listen to the *Relaxation Training* for the full 21 days! – it's just not worth the risk not to do it properly.

How 'The Relaxation Training Exercise' Will Help You Achieve Control of Your Subconscious:

The ***Relaxation Training Exercise*** is a *'guided relaxation'* which will help you to relax physically and mentally. As your body relaxes, your *Mind* will naturally shift into its own relaxed state, which is at about 10 cps and well *Centered* within your *Subconscious Mind*. Then, as your *Mind* continues to relax, your thoughts will begin to gently slow down to almost a *"dream-like"* sensation.

As this dream-like sensation increases, your awareness of your physical body will generally decrease and you will start becoming more aware and focused on only the thoughts and mental images you are experiencing. It is at this time that you are functioning within your *Subconscious Level*. Seems easy, doesn't it? **And it is ...**

The only things you will need to do to gain extraordinary mastery over your *Subconscious* is to have the desire to relax and the willingness to listen to the *Relaxation Training*. In so doing, you will develop the habit of relaxation which will allow you to achieve the same ideal state of relaxation on your own, without the use of the MP3 recording.

A Few Important Things to Remember Before You Begin:

As there is no way you can make a mistake, don't try to relax! Just let it happen. You're not being tested and there is no one watching you as to how you respond -- so don't start judging and analyzing your own experience. Further, there is no right or wrong way to 'feel' when you are relaxed. Some people find that their bodies begin to feel extremely light, as if it could float away, while others experience their bodies becoming comfortably heavy. It doesn't matter! Some people report that they totally lose themselves in the relaxation, as if they were in some type of 'dream world'. Others find that even though they are relaxed, they remain mildly aware of sounds and movements around them. Once again, it simply doesn't matter! Everyone experiences deep relaxation differently.

If for any reason, you find yourself over-relaxing and dozing off to sleep during the *"Relaxation Training"*, this usually indicates that you are extremely tired due to lack of sleep. However, if dozing off to sleep during the relaxation becomes a regular occurrence, it will be necessary for you to start asking yourself *"Why am I avoiding learning how to master my mind?"* We are serious. Unless you are truly physically exhausted, (in which case you need to embed the *"Quality Sleep Technique"* as soon as possible), some part of you is resisting taking charge of your life and it will be important that you discover the reason for your resistance.

In the meantime though, you can prevent yourself from falling asleep during *"The Relaxation Training"*, by saying to yourself before you begin, *"I will not fall asleep and I will* remain *totally alert throughout the "Relaxation Training."*

If we must be honest, we have often found that those who had the tendency to fall asleep during the relaxation were doing so simply because of *"mental laziness"* and not because of some deep inner resistance. Obviously, they felt it was a lot easier to just let their thoughts wander and drift (often to sleep) rather than to take charge and keep their thoughts focused on *"The Relaxation Training."* Inevitably though, when these individuals finally admitted to themselves that this was the issue, their tendency to fall asleep during *The Relaxation* nearly always stopped immediately.

If you do find your *Mind* wandering during the guided relaxation, then gently bring your thoughts back and refocus them on what you are doing. Wandering thoughts are a natural occurrence, especially in the beginning and chances are that up until now, your thoughts were allowed to wander whenever and wherever they please. Now, however, you cannot afford to let them just wander but rather you need to take control of your thoughts if you are to achieve the quality life you desire.

Always remember though, bring your thoughts back gently. The purpose of *"The Relaxation Training"* is to learn to relax and not to create any additional stress. The best way to do that is to simply become *relaxed about being relaxed* ... okay!

If your eyes open during the relaxation, that's fine -- simply close them and continue with the *Relaxation Training* when you are ready.

We should point out that there is a reason and purpose for each part of *The Relaxation Training Exercise*. Therefore, it is very important that you participate in each part of *The Relaxation*. The following will explain the purpose of the various parts that comprise *"The Relaxation Training Exercise"*:

Learning to Relax Your Body:

Initially, you will be directed to relax various parts of your body: the feet, the legs, abdominal area, the chest area, the arms, the shoulder muscles, the neck muscles, as well as the head and face area. During your 21 day training, it is essential that you take the time to specifically relax these various parts of your body. It is understandable that after a few days, you might begin to merely *'play'* the *"Relaxation Training Exercise"* rather than to actually be listening to it and allowing yourself to *'actively participate'* in the body relaxation. By not actively participating, you will be denying yourself the opportunity to master physical relaxation on your own in the future. So be sure to allow yourself to experience the full body relaxation each time you listen to *"The Relaxation Exercise Training."* By doing so, you will learn to achieve full body relaxation very quickly and easily.

If during this full body relaxation you become aware of a specific area of your body that is resisting relaxation, make mental note of that area of the body, as it indicates that significant stress and tension are residing within that area. As the *MP3* recording will not allow you to stop and work on that area before proceeding, it is recommended that you return to that part of the body on your own to help release the tension and stress that are being stored there.

By practicing full body relaxation for the 21 days, you will gain the ability to relax your body quickly and easily whenever you desire in the future. Besides releasing tension and stress from your body, it will provide you outstanding benefits health-wise. As we are sure you know, tension and stress can cause significant health problems and aggravate many pre-existing health problems as well. Lastly, relaxing the body is a very enjoyable experience. So give yourself the opportunity to enjoy the pleasure.

Learning to Relax Your Mind:

Just as important as it is to relax the body, you also need to learn how to relax your *Mind*. Normally you are not aware of your *Mind's* hyperactivity or *"Mind Chatter"*. It is only when you begin to relax, such as when you are going to sleep or daydreaming, that you tend to become aware of the endless stream of thoughts that are passing through your *Mind*. It is essential that you learn to *'Mind Your Mind'* by learning to quiet its hyperactivity and chatter when required.

To help you relax your *Mind*, the *'Relaxation Training'* incorporates a few mini-techniques for mastering *Mind* relaxation. One of these mini-techniques will be when you are asked to imagine yourself walking down 10 steps and counting from 10-1 while doing so. This is similar to counting backwards when being anesthetized before surgery. Counting backwards, rather than forward, requires the *Mind*   to   maintain somewhat more focus and attention. By focusing on the numbers in this manner, you will easily learn to stop the *"Mind Chatter"* that normally never seems to stop.

The Relaxation also provides another mini-technique for *Mind* relaxation, *"The Valley of Relaxation"* which requires your *Mind* to imagine *a* beautiful valley, on a beautiful summer day. For most people, the thought of a beautiful valley tends to conjure up feelings of peacefulness and quietness -- which are the exact feelings you want to bring to your *Mind* to help it relax. As your *Mind* begins to imagine this valley, you will help it stay focused by directing your *Mind* to use its *inner-senses* of sight, sound, smell, taste and touch to imagine this valley in detail. By taking control of your *Mind's inner-senses,* you are in fact taking *'control of your Mind'* itself. By gaining control, you will be able to easily relax your *Mind* even more by directing it to imagine that you are relaxing, perhaps in the shade of a tree, lying in the tall grass or relaxing near a creek or stream.

The purpose behind this *'Valley of Relaxation'* is quite simple: when your *Mind* relaxes, your body relaxes -- and when your *Mind* and body relax, your brain frequencies *'naturally'* slow down and tend to level off at about 10 cps -- which is precisely in the midrange of the *Alpha Level* of your *Subconscious.*

In short, if to reach your *Subconscious* you need to master relaxation, both physically and mentally, and the *"Relaxation Training Exercise"* is designed to help you learn to do just that. Makes sense? Good!

What You May Experience:

When you are asked to imagine your *'Valley of Relaxation'* with "*trees, flowers, a creek or stream (with flowing, clear water) and snowcapped mountains*" some of you will imagine a valley so real that you will be able to even sense the fragrance of the flowers and the coolness of the water. For others, when asked to imagine this valley, all you might experience is "*total darkness, nothing but darkness*" -- no pictures, no images. Our response is, great!

"*What!*" You may be asking. Well, let us explain. Some people are "*internal visualizers*" and they usually have little difficulty *'seeing things'* in their *Minds*. Others are more naturally *'internal feelers'*, and as such, when they close their eyes, they tend to *'feel or/sense'* that things are there but usually don't actually *'see anything'* – no pictures nor images.

While the majority of people seem to be, at least to some degree, both *'visualizers'* and *'feelers'*, trust us when we say, it really, really doesn't matter how you sense/experience your *Subconscious Realm*! We have no vested interest in trying to sweet talk you or to appease you when we say this. It's just that people vary in the way they experience their *'Inner Realm'* and however you experience yours, will be perfect for you!

We surely appreciate that you would love to have the *'complete multimedia version'* of seeing and feeling, but we can only say that you can equate it to the difference between one person having blue eyes and another having brown. The color of a person's eyes isn't what's really important. What is important is that the eyes work. In the same way, we as human beings vary as to how we perceive our *Inner Realm*. The only thing that is important is not how you experience your *inner realm* ... but how well you're able to use your *Inner Realm* to achieve significant results in your life.

After working with close to 10,000 people during our combined 40 years of teaching seminars, neither one of us has ever found that being a *'feeler'* versus being a *'visualizer'* within the *Inner Realm*, had made one iota of difference to any person's ability to achieve maximum success. What did make a difference was the person's sincere desire to be successful in his/her life and the belief that he/she could do so. We can't say it any clearer, could we? So stop worrying, stop thinking, stop analyzing and simply let yourself relax and enjoy your *Inner Realm*. Got it? Good!

So as you go through the *guided relaxation*, allow yourself to discover (not judge), how you personally perceive and sense your *Inner Realm*. And whatever you do discover, will provide you invaluable self-understanding as to how you can best program your goals and desires in the future at the *Inner Realms* of your *Subconscious*.

Moving on … after the *"Valley of Relaxation"*, you will be asked to repeat to yourself various beneficial statements. These beneficial statements are often referred to as 'Affirmations.' A detailed explanation of the purpose and benefits of *Affirmations* will be discussed later. For now however, let us give you a hint as to why they are so important. Let us just say -- *"If you hear something often enough … you'll believe it."*

Lastly, if at any time during the relaxation, you start feeling *"you're not doing something perfectly"* or *"you should be able to do it better,"* you are beginning to *analyze* your experience rather than *participating* in it, which is a function of your *Conscious Mind* and not of your *Subconscious Mind*. If this happens, simply acknowledge that you are analyzing, and when you are ready, take a deep breath and refocus your thoughts on the *Guided Relaxation*. No Harm Done.

Please Note:

This would be a good time to take a break from reading and actually listen to *"The Relaxation Training Exercise"* if you haven't begun to do so already.

When you are finished listening, you may desire to simply remain quiet for a while before returning to reading the book. Whatever you decide, it is fine, so go with your feelings! Be assured, we will be waiting for you.

Quality Life Training

AFFIRMATIONS:

BE CAREFUL WHAT YOU SAY ...
YOUR WORDS MAY COME BACK
TO HAUNT YOU

The purpose of stating and repeating the various *Beneficial Statements* as was done during the *"The Relaxation Training Exercise"*, is based on a very elementary principle: *"If you* hear *something often enough ... you'll believe it."* It would follow that by saying, even flippantly, to yourself that *"You can't do anything right"* -- you are actually telling your *Subconscious* to *"ensure that you will make some mistake so as not to do things correctly."* Are we suggesting that by saying or just thinking the statement *"I can't do anything right"* you *could be* preventing yourself from succeeding at something you truly desire? *Yes we are!* We are not, however, suggesting that by saying or thinking that statement, will guarantee that you will fail. What we said was that it *"could"* prevent you from succeeding. Therefore, you need to understand and remember the rules (*the rules of engagement*) that govern giving commands to your *Subconscious:*

1. If you say something often enough, your *Subconscious* will accept it as true. Once embedded in your *Subconscious* as true, your *Subconscious Mind* will act on it accordingly.

43

2. If what you are affirming has any attached emotional factor, that *Affirmation* will be embed even faster and deeper within the *Subconscious* and its influence on your future thinking and behavior will be greatly intensified.

3. Regardless of the actual intended meaning of an *Affirmation,* the *Subconscious* will interpret it literally and act accordingly.

We are hesitant to make too big of an issue of the importance of watching what you think and say to yourself. Our hesitancy is because we don't want you to become paranoid about saying something, in fear that it could unintentionally create unwanted dramas and problems in your life. If you were beginning to think that way, then please stop. Your *Subconscious Mind* is not stupid or so totally vulnerable. Words have no power in and of themselves -- any power they do have is derived from the emotional feeling that you have learned to associate with that word or words. Simply said, words themselves have no power -- it is the power you, or others give them, that will determine the impact that they can have.

If someone says to you *"I think you're one, big flitying"* -- what would be your reaction? Would you be offended or flattered? Would you be hurt or angry? We doubt any of these, as we doubt that you have any clue as to what *'flitying'* means (by the way, nor do we). So once again, words in themselves have no meaning or power except that which we have given them. Any *'impact'* that a word(s) has on us or others has been *'learned'*.

Further, the same word can impact totally differently depending on the culture in which it is spoken, even though the cultures speak the same language. In one culture a word is totally acceptable and in another, a child will have his/her mouth washed out with soap for saying it. The phrase, *"I'll knock you up,'* has a totally different connotation in England, then it does in the USA. In England, it simply means, *"knock on your door until you wake up and answer it".*

In the USA, however, it has just a slightly different meaning, which is, *"I'm going to make you pregnant."* Well okay, perhaps it's more than just a slight difference in meaning, but the point is, it's the same language but its meaning and impact can be totally different!

This of course is not only true for English but for Spanish as well. When Elena was lecturing in Spanish to a group in Miami, she said to those attending that *"A mother was nursing* her *"wawa"*.

Most of the people in the room first looked somewhat startled and then some started to giggle. Perhaps you should be reminded that Elena is from Chile, where the word '*wawa*' means '*baby*' -- yet nearly everyone in her Miami seminar was Cuban. To them the word '*wawa*' meant '*bus*' - so they heard *"A mother was nursing* her *bus"* ... same word, same language yet two totally different meanings. Silly isn't it? It may be silly, but very significant, nonetheless. Do you see where this is leading? Apply this to *Affirmations* and to self-communication and perhaps you might begin to understand why we must be careful as to what we say and think.

Imagine that you are the '*Lecturer*' and your *Subconscious Mind* is your '*Audience*'. If your objective is to communicate with your audience, common sense would say that you will need to speak to them in *"their language"* and use words in a way that your audience (in this case, your *Subconscious Mind*) will understand. It doesn't matter what you, as the lecturer, (your *Conscious Mind*) means. It is what your audience (your *Subconscious Mind*) hears and understands. So in regards to what you think and say to yourself ... choose your words carefully!

What You Need to Know About Communicating With Your *Subconscious Mind*

Keep It Literal: When it comes to communicating with your *Subconscious*, always remember that it always takes things *literally* versus *figuratively*. Let us explain this, as it is important.

As a general rule, adults process language figuratively, while children tend to process language literally. There is a classic example of this that both of us heard years ago. In essence it goes as follows:'

A mother simply said to her son, who was about six years of age, *"I'm going to step out for a while so watch the food on the stove while I'm gone."*

When the mother returned a short while later, she was greeted with the smell of smoke and burning food. She immediately rushed to the kitchen, only to find her son sitting on a small chair, staring at the pot on the stove which was billowing smoke from the food burning inside. When confronted, her son simply said, *"Mommy you told me I should watch the food. I am!"*

Another story of taking things literally, happened a few years ago in a small café in the center of Sydney. While Tom was waiting for his food, he noticed a young Japanese couple sitting at a table near him. They were behaving in what he thought was somewhat of a strange manner. They would both switch from looking at a sign on the wall, to looking at the underside of their empty plates. This went on for a short while, when suddenly the young man, who had noticed that Tom was watching, leaned over and asked him, in somewhat broken English, if Tom could explain something that was confusing them. The source of the confusion was that the sign on the wall said *"Homemade Dishes"* while the bottom of their plates said *"Made in China."*

The problem was quite simple. As they were learning a new language, English in this case, they were naturally taking everything *'literally'* that they read.

Both of these stories are perfect examples of the confusion that can so easily exist when our *Conscious Mind* (which communicates figuratively) attempts to communicate with our *Subconscious Mind* (which communicates literally). Therefore, when stating your *Affirmations, be as literal* as possible to ensure that your *Subconscious* fully understands what you desire.

Keep It Simple: Don't babble -- keep your *affirmations* short, sweet and to the point. More than once, students have asked us to review the *Affirmations* that they had written. In a few cases, some of them had nearly written a short story. An *Affirmation* is meant to be *a statement* -- not a dissertation. Besides, as you will need to repeat that *Affirmation* to yourself several times, a long-winded *Affirmation* will simply become unworkable and lose its impact.

Make It Positive: Another very important factor when creating an effective *Affirmation* is *"make it positive."* Rather than saying. *"I don't want to be sick,"* say. *"I am in perfect health."* Instead of *"I don't want to be* *poor,"* convert it to a positive statement: *"I am prosperous and financially secure."* The reason for this is based on how the *Subconscious* processes the information it receives.

To help you understand this principle, we are going to ask you **_not to do_** something and that is:

Do Not Think Of A Pink Elephant!

Well, what just came to your *Mind?* Chances are you just thought of a *Pink Elephant,* even though you were asked specifically not to do so. In order not to think of something, your *Subconscious Mind* has to first think about something before it can stop thinking about it. What's the point? The point is, if you choose to repeat the Affirmation *"I don't want to be sick",* your *Subconscious Mind* will have to first imagine *you being sick* (thereby embedding in your *Subconscious* that you are sick) before it can stop thinking about it. Just as your *Mind* had to first think of a **pink elephant** before it could *not think of it.*

Applying this to your *Affirmations,* remember that instead of telling your *Subconscious* <u>what you don't want</u>, tell it precisely <u>what you do want</u>. So instead of saying *"I don't want to be sick,"* it would be better to say *"I am in good health.",* which is precisely what you do want.

Conclusion: Say what you really want in the first place and prevent any unnecessary confusion.

Quality Life Training

YOUR BELIEFS AND
DESIRES

If you are serious about living a rich and fulfilling life, you must fully understand the role and the power that your **beliefs** and **desires** have in determining the quality of your health, happiness and well-being.

Understanding the Power of Beliefs

To help you understand the power of your *beliefs,* we will now take the time to explore the nature of *beliefs* and why they have such power in determining the quality of your life and why their power must never be underestimated.

Firstly, any statement you hear, regardless if it is actually <u>true or not</u>, can become embedded in your *Subconscious* as a *belief* that will be considered to be <u>absolutely true</u>. Your *Subconscious Mind* does not have the ability to distinguish between what is true and what is false or what is real from what is not. That is an exclusive function of your *Conscious Mind.* This fact that any statement, once embedded in the *Subconscious,* is considered to be absolutely true, gives that statement tremendous power.

In each of these cases, the *Subconscious* would have accepted something it heard or read as *'true'* without any actual proof that it was true. Further, it will act on what it now *'knows'* to be *true,* regardless of the consequences. Think about how many lives have been ruined, how many relationships torn apart and how many careers destroyed simply because of *rumors, gossip* or *hearsay* -- which were merely statements heard but accepted by the *Subconscious* as *"gospel truth."* Scary, isn't it? So, never underestimate the power of *"Beliefs"* (whether they are yours or others) as they can become a mighty, destructive force to be reckoned with.

The Truth of It All:

It's important to remember that *truth* has nothing to do with any of this. Your *Subconscious Mind,* as we have said, accepts everything embedded within its domain as *'true'*, whether it is or not. Further, it has been estimated that <u>99%</u> of everything we, as human beings hold to be true, is actually based on a mere *"belief"* that the *Subconscious* has come to accept as true.

Take a moment and consider that there are very few things that any of us really, really *"know"* for sure. Nearly everything we may think is *'true'* is actually only a *'belief* that we believe is true. We are being very serious when we make this statement. Consider the following: You most probably believe that the earth is round, don't you? Do you however actually *"know"* that for sure? Isn't it a fact that you personally, have never actually seen the Earth from space? Rather you have come to accept/believe that the earth is round, based only on what you have been told by others. Sure you've seen the pictures -- Hollywood studios can create magic today, can't they? So unless you have personally traveled into space and personally viewed this planet from that great distance, you really couldn't say, with absolute certainty that the earth is in fact round. Could you? The only *truth* you know for sure in regards to the earth being round, is that you *'believe'* it is, rather than actually *'knowing'* that it is. Are we right? Not sure, then let's try another one ...

If we asked you if you had a physical, beating heart, you would most probably say that of course you do. Then let me ask you, *'How do you know for sure?' Have you seen it?* We mean, have you personally really, really ever seen your own heart or are you just assuming that you *'must'* have one because you were told that everyone does. Some will say *"Of course I have a heart, I saw x-rays of my chest area."* But again, how do you know, without any shadow of doubt, that the x-ray you were shown was actually yours? You don't!

We are not being ludicrous when we asked these questions ... what we are trying to do is point out that there is a very significant and important distinction that exists between *"actually knowing something is true"* versus merely *"believing something is* true." We admit that often there is a very, very fine line that distinguishes a *truth* from a *belief*, but it's an important distinction, nevertheless.

Ask yourself, what do you absolutely, positively, without a shadow of doubt, know for sure about anything? Chances are you would have to answer very little. In fact, the only things that perhaps you absolutely, positively might know for sure are only those things that you have personally experienced. Everything else, and we mean _everything else_, is based on a *belief* that it is *true*. Further, even the things you have personally experienced could be suspect, as is often the case when a number of people report totally different scenarios regarding a car accident.

This is a really awesome insight when you think about it and if we lost you, please read and reread the previous paragraphs until you are comfortable with the difference between *"knowing something is true"* and *"believing something is true."* Once you've *"Got It"* it can make your whole life a whole lot simpler, as you will be able to start distinguishing what is *"really real and true"* from what you were *"assuming and believing"* to be true."

It is usually at this point that we often have received a rebuttal to this type of querying, along the lines of: *"Well, there are some things that are simply scientific facts, such as, that the earth is round."* Scientific Facts? Please understand something, when it comes to science: all divisions of science generally spend a good part of their time either **1)** developing new theories (which is another word for beliefs) or **2)** Proving or challenging their old ones.

What was 'true' yesterday is often replaced by a new 'belief/theory' today, What were considered absolute truths 500 years ago are today considered as *'primitive'* and sometimes *'superstitious'* understanding of basic astronomy, biology, etc. Was it not, since the beginning of time, *believed* that the sun went around the earth, and that belief was held *'true'* until only a few hundred years ago? Then one day, someone decided to challenge that *'truth,'* and Galileo was not only scorned and ridiculed by the scientific community of his time but he was charged with heresy by the Church as well.

Truth vs Beliefs in Regards to Who You Are:

Now that we have discussed the fine line that exists between what is really *'true'* and what is just *'a belief,'* we must now ask *"What do you know for sure about who you are and what you're capable of?"* Well? To find out, take a sheet of paper and start writing a list of:

1. **All the Things You Are:** hard-working, diligent, responsible, clever, etc. and then write down all the things:

2. **All the Things You're Capable Of:** being a good mother or father, being a loving wife/husband, being a good employee, being wealthy, being a good friend, being a good cook, being a good musician, etc.

Then, when you have completed the list, simply write after each item -- either:

1. **'I absolutely know this for sure because (state how you know it's absolutely true):** o r

2. **'I'm not really sure this is true, but I believe or think it's true (state why you don't know this is absolutely true):**

Remember, you might desperately *want to believe* something you wrote about yourself as being true but the time has come to start *"Being Absolutely Truthful"* with yourself. So if you're not sure why you believe something about yourself is true, then simply admit it, no harm will done, we promise. Rather, your life will stop being an illusion and you will start living your life based on the solid ground of truth. Besides, no one likes being deceived and lied to -- so why would you want to deceive and lie to yourself!

If you truly desire to live the rest of your life being who you truly are, then remember that it is your *Subconscious* that contains the *'blueprint'* to create the future you desire. It will be crucial for you to check out that *'blueprint'* to ensure that your future will be built to your specifications. Specifically, you will need to seek out and destroy any *'fundamental beliefs'* that may prevent you from achieving the life you desire. As an example, if you are holding a *'fundamental belief'* that *"money is the root of all evil,"* your *Subconscious* belief system will do everything it can to keep money from manifesting in your life. And, if financial abundance does somehow find its way into your life, your *Subconscious* will do everything in its power to get rid of it ASAP. How often have you heard of people who have won large amounts of money and lost it all within a very short period of time? They weren't in debt when they won the money but suddenly they're filing for bankruptcy.

In the same way, if you have an embedded *'fundamental belief'* that you are *"unlovable"*, the chances are very slim that you would ever be able to form a long-term *"loving relationship"* with another person. With such a belief, your *Subconscious* will work very hard to prevent any person who expresses love for you from coming into your life, let alone staying. From the *Subconscious* point of view, it is in essence saying, *"We know we're unlovable and therefore, if a person says they love you, they are either lying, trying to deceive you or they are very stupid. In any case, we must not have anything to do with that person."* So for the umpteenth time, *"You are what you believe you are."* So take charge of what your *Subconscious* beliefs and you will be taking charge of your life.

Embedding Beliefs:

There are many factors that determine how readily any belief finds a permanent resting place in the *Subconscious*. There are no hard and fast rules that can be established that would hold true for every type of *'belief.'* However, generally speaking, there are two significant factors that strongly influence how quickly and/or how easily a *'belief'* will be embedded:

1. **The Source** of the *'New Belief.'*

2. **The Importance** of the *'New Belief'* to the individual.

In regards to *"The Source,"* it will rely on another *underlining belief* that usually will determine how quickly a *'new belief'* is accepted and embedded. This underlining belief is what the *Subconscious believes'* is the *source* from which the *'new belief'* was obtained.

It All Starts in Childhood ...

Generally for a young child, whatever is said by his/her *"Authority Figure(s),"* parents, teachers and adults in general, will be accepted as *'absolute truth'* almost instantaneously i.e. *"My teacher said..."* In regards to this point, there is the Jesuit priests' adage that says, *'Give me a child until he is seven, and I will give you the man.'* A similar one can be found within the *Hitler Youth Movement*, which was based on Adolf Hitler's belief that the future of Nazi Germany was its children. It says, *'Get the children when they're young and you will control them ... their minds can't say no.'*

The question you might be asking is, *"Why are children so vulnerable?"* Simple, children generally do not have the ability to accept or reject ideas, beliefs or negative statements, especially those that come from their *"Authority Figure(s)."* Their ability to accept or reject will only start when their analytical and reasoning skills *(Conscious Mind)* develop. And that development generally only slowly begins around the age of 6-7 (therefore the Jesuits adage) and generally it is not fully developed until around the age of *14-16*.

Yet this principle that *"the source of a belief helps* determine *how fast a belief will be embedded,"* is by no means limited to children. As an adult, your parents and your former teachers most probably are no longer your ultimate *"Authority Figure(s)."* Instead, your source of *'absolute truth'* may now be what you read in newspapers, hear on TV/radio or hear from people you trust and consider your *Authority Figure(s)*.

A classic and a powerful example of this was the broadcasting of *'War of the Worlds'*, by Orson Welles in 1938. This simulation of a radio news broadcast (created with voice acting and sound effects) caused a portion of the USA listening audience (around 25%) to conclude that what they were hearing was *'an actual news account of an invasion from Mars'*. The mass hysteria was so high that people began running into the streets, fleeing the cities in their cars, hiding in cellars, loading their guns, and some were even wrapping their heads in wet towels to protect themselves from the Martian's poison gas. Some people were reported to have told the police and newspapers that they had personally *"witnessed"* the invasion.

Nothing has changed since 1938, has it? If people see or hear something from their *'Authority Figure(s)'* (newspapers, television, certain colleagues, friends & neighbors) -- they will often believe it without questioning its *'truth'*. It is for this reason that governments use the media whenever possible, such as with *"Press Conferences"* to convey the *'real truth'* to their constituents. Local and Federal governments will immediately set up a *"Rumor Hotline"* to dispel any false information when some significant emergency develops. Having said this, you can now get a better understanding of how some of the beliefs you might hold to be *'absolutely true'* in regards to *who you* are and your *abilities,* might have been only based on mere *"rumors."* Rumors often spread unintentionally and unknowingly by parents, teachers and others people you trusted the most when you were a child.

Unfortunately though, some of these *'rumors'* you heard about yourself became embedded as *beliefs* in your *Subconscious*. It may have been such as: *"You'll* never *amount to anything"* -*"You can't do anything right"* - *"You're such a bad child, God's going to punish you"* - *"Life's tough, so don't expect too much from it"* - *"You're just like your father and we know he's no good."* and this list could go on, and on, and on.

The problem is, unless you have updated such deep-seeded beliefs, your *Subconscious* is still holding those same *beliefs* about *whom and what you* are now, as it did when you were a child. And even though you obviously see yourself differently now as an adult, don't for a moment fool yourself into thinking that those beliefs aren't still influencing (often in very subtle ways) the way you see and feel about yourself. Further, and perhaps more importantly, these beliefs, regardless of how irrational they might be, *will never change* ... well not on their own at least.

In order to change them, your only option will be to decide to delve into your own *Subconscious Mind* and make the necessary changes yourself. As daunting as that task might seem to be, it really isn't. Learning to change *'beliefs'* found within your *Subconscious* is exactly what you are learning to do right now as you read through this book and listen to the MP3 recordings! We are not suggesting that you are being forced to change by reading this book or listening to the MP3 recordings. It will always remain your choice. If you decide not to change or modify any of your *'Disempowering'* beliefs in your *Subconscious*, just remember that there's nobody else can do it for you. It's your *Mind* and only you can change it ... and that's the way it should be! Right?

Beware of Unintentionally Creating New Disempowering Beliefs:

Be honest, do you tend to think or say to yourself any *'Disempowering Statements?'* If you do, be aware that they can easily become embedded *Disempowering Beliefs* in your *Subconscious*. Some examples of *Disempowering Statements* might be: *"Damn, I can't do anything right.", "Nothing good ever happens to me.", "I never get what I want.", "I'll never find the right person.",* etc., etc. -- simple statements that are often said without thinking about their implications. It will be extremely important that you start becoming aware what you're thinking in order to discover if you are making any *'Disempowering Statements'* that could become *'Disempowering Beliefs.'* If *Disempowering Beliefs* are allowed to become embedded and remain in your *Subconscious*, your life can, and most probably will, become nothing but an ongoing battle, filled with constant conflicts and disappointments. Achieving what you really desire will be more often by **chance** than by **choice**. As soon as one problem has been dealt with in your life, another will quickly surface, resulting in you spending your life solving problems rather than enjoying it. How sad!

How dramatic, you say and how right you would be. Don't be fooled, however, into thinking that you might be immune to these treacherous little *Disempowering Beliefs... because* you're not. Regardless of how you might want to think that *"you have it all together"*, chances are a few of these *Disempowering Self-Beliefs* are securely tucked away deep within you, deep within your *Subconscious Mind*. Perhaps they are lying dormant now, but some unforeseen event in the future might just possibly re-activate them again. Since you most probably would not know whether or not you are harboring such beliefs, we urge you not to take a chance but rather take the time to seek them out and destroy them ASAP.

How? Simple! Start embedding and reinforcing *Empowering Beliefs* that will deactivate any pre-existing *'Disempowering'* ones. You might be pleased to know that, if you have been listening to the **Relaxation Training Exercise** on a regular basis, you have already begun your "*Seek & Destroy Mission*". The *Affirmations* that you repeat during the *Relaxation Training Exercise* are in fact, *Empowering Affirmations:* i.e. empowering you by affirming your success & prosperity, health, self-image (how you see yourself), and your overall self-esteem (how you feel about yourself) amongst other things. It must be said again, *'You Are What You Believe You Are'* and hopefully now you will believe it.

REMEMBER ...

All Of Your Beliefs Are TRUE
To Your Subconscious:

Whatever you believe you are -- is true. So, if you believe you are limited -- *you are!* If you believe you are unlimited in what you can achieve and do -- *you are!* As mentioned numerous time before, to your *Subconscious Mind,* all beliefs that you have fed it will be used as the **Master Blueprint** from which the quality of your life will be built.

Note: You can't have it both ways -- if on one hand you believe you're "*unlovable*" and on the other hand, you desperately desire "*To be in a love relationship*" -- the *belief* wins out over your *desire* and you will need to buy a puppy. Sorry!

Regarding Your Desires:

Now that we have discussed *'Beliefs',* it is time to discuss another part of the "*Success Puzzle*", namely, *'Desire'*. If you really, really want/ desire something, and you are willing to do whatever it takes to get it, what can stop you?" We would say, probably nothing, except a belief that you might have that getting what you want would cause you a *whole lot of problems*. Regardless of how strongly you may **Desire** something, if you have an underlining belief that getting what you desire will cause you severe pain and suffering, chances are you will lose your **desire** (by losing your motivation) to pursue it.

Example:

You desire to have a certain car. You also have a **belief** that "*The only way you could have that kind of car, would be to steal it and then you would probably go to jail for stealing it.*" Chances are, the *belief* you have that you will be punished severely would most likely override your *desire* to have that car. Pretty basic, isn't it?

So What Are Your Options?

Option 1: You could attempt to stop desiring that type of car and set your *Mind* to a car you could easily afford. Unfortunately, by doing so you will have compromised your *Desire* and it is almost always impossible to be highly motivated when you have compromised anything.

Option 2: You could attempt to change the belief within yourself that you would be punished is you were caught stealing the car and thereby eliminate this dilemma. Unfortunately, just because you changed your belief that you won't be punished, does not change the reality in the courts of law.

Option 3: Another possibility would be to change/override your belief that "*The only way you could have that kind of car would be to steal it*". Instead, you could embed a new belief that states: "*If I work hard and save my money, I would develop good credit. Then I could have that car.*" -- **Bingo!**

You have just found another way to solve this puzzle. Sure, it will mean you have to work and save your money. It also means that you can have your dream car without having to go to jail. Changing a "*belief*" can change the outcome drastically. If your beliefs can be *Disempowering* and prevent you from getting what you *Desire*, they can also provide you *Empowering* solutions to otherwise unobtainable dreams.

The Emotional Aspect of Desires:

The *belief* that *'If you get your car you would be punished'*, has at its essence an issue regarding *"Fear."* Anytime *"Fear,"* or for that matter any *negative emotions,* is involved in the puzzle to succeed, the *negative emotions* will always win out, even if you have to lose out. This is simply your *"Survival Instinct"* at work,

If you have a strong *fear* of taking responsibility or being held responsible for your actions, your *desire* to become a *"Managing Director"* most probably will never happen. We say this because by the very nature of being a *Managing Director* would require a person to be responsible for his/her department. Now, if you could eliminate *'your fear'* of taking responsibility, it would drastically shift the possibility of you becoming a *Managing Director* from nearly impossible to very possible.

How does one do that? How does one *'Deactivate a 'fear' of taking responsibility?'* This can be easily achieved by applying the same procedure we explored earlier when we were discussing how to overcome the fear of talking in front of a group people. Begin by embedding a new belief that would affirm that *you are a responsible person, i.e. "I am a responsible person and I am comfortable taking responsibility for my life."*

Now start embedding and reinforcing that in your *Subconscious* for a few weeks and then start programming again to get that position as *"Managing Director."* It's not difficult. It's just a matter of whether or not you are ready to do what is needed to make the mental changes to get what you want.

From our experience, the emotion of *fear* is perhaps one of the most common barriers to achieving what we really desire. Remember, *"fear"* comes in many forms and degrees. It could be the *"fear of being successful"* or the *"fear of being loved"* or the *"fear of not being good enough and ultimately to be rejected"* and the list goes on and on.

The Message Here is Simple:

Find your fears and the corresponding *Self-defeating & Disempowering Beliefs* -- and purge them from your *Subconscious!* Unless they are eliminated, they will continue to set you up to *lose* ... to lose having that relationship, that car, that job, etc., that you so strongly desire. Keep losing and you will keep reinforcing your *Sense of Fear* and your *Self-defeating* and *Disempowering Belief* that you are inadequate and/or unworthy to have the things you desire in your life. *Fear* and *Self-defeating Beliefs* are simply destructive, dangerous and devious. They must be sought out and destroyed as they are **Terrorists** within your soul and bent on bringing you down.

So now it is left to you as to whether or not you desire to free yourself of any *'Disempowering Beliefs'*, regardless of their source, that are preventing you from living the life of empowerment and quality you so rightly deserve. And if you desire to live *a life of quality,* then get on with it. Start making changes in your *Subconscious* by eliminating the *beliefs* that are holding you back from achieving what you desire and embedding those that will take you forward.

To do so, continue listening to the *Relaxation Training Exercise* in order to embed and reinforce *Empowering Beliefs* and *deactivate* those that are *Disempowering* you. There's a wonderful world waiting for you. All you have to do is desire to claim it.

It is now time for you to start opening *a few the door* and windows of your *Subconscious Mind* and begin cleaning up. It will begin with throwing out the rubbish - the rubbish of *Disempowering Beliefs* and *Counterproductive Habits.* Then, with the tools and techniques that you will soon have, you will be able to start rebuilding your life, your health, your wealth and your happiness. Need we say more? So let's start with the tools and techniques that you will need to build your future and change your life.

Enjoy! **Tom & Elena**

PART 2

THE TOOLS AND TECHNIQUES
FOR ACHIEVING A QUALITY LIFE:

As we proceed with introducing a variety of techniques for your benefit, the following points become your responsibility in order to make these tools/techniques useful and beneficial in your life.

1. You *must* sincerely *desire/want* the skill or technique.

2. You *must* reinforce *that skill* or technique at least 2-3 times by listening to the **Embedding Techniques** MP3.

3. You must avoid negating that skill or technique by avoiding reinforcing any contrary thoughts, such as, *"I can't do that"*, *"It won't work for me"* or *"It's too* easy & *simple,"* ... **and that's it!**

Some Additional Points:

When it is said that you must sincerely *desire/want something,* it means just that. An approach of *"Oh, that sounds interesting, perhaps I should try that* one" is usually not sufficient for the skill/technique to be properly embedded in your *Subconscious.* Wishy-washy personal development will be just that, wishy-washy, halfhearted and lacking the intensity of desire required to bring about the changes in your life. Got that? Good!

PLEASE NOTE: The tools/techniques that we have provided to help you build the life you truly desire, are those that we have found are essential '*all-purpose tools*' that any good '*builder*' should have.

We have made a sincere effort to organize these skills/tools so that they can be easily obtained when necessary. Some tools/techniques, such as "*The Relaxation Trigger*" and "*Goal-Setting and Problem-Solving*" will most probably be used more often. Other tools/techniques, such as the technique for *Eliminating Headaches,* might be used less frequently ... hopefully. Regardless, your toolbox will be very complete and will be more than adequate to enhance and/or repair most aspects of your life.

So let's begin . . .

THE RELAXATION TRIGGER

There will be many uses far the ***Relaxation Trigger Technique*** in your day-to-day life. Anytime you experience feelings such as nervousness, irritability, anxiousness, anger, etc., *and* you do not desire to have these feelings, simply use your ***Relaxation Trigger Technique.*** The purpose of this technique is not to suppress your feelings and reactions but rather to allow you to take control of them.

PLEASE NOTE: If you have been listening to the *"Relaxation Exercise Training",* this technique will have already been embedded in your *Subconscious and is* ready *for your use.*

The Purpose:

The purpose is to *'trigger'* your body and *Mind* to relax quickly and easily whenever you desire to do so. It is one of the few techniques that does not require you to be at a relaxed level of *Mind* in order to use it effectively.

This 'simple' technique has a wide variety of practical benefits that you can use on a daily basis.

- You're becoming overwhelmed with tension and stress and you want to *"calm down and relax."*

- You're at a staff meeting but when your boss calls on you for information, your *Mind* goes blank.

- You're giving a talk to a small or large group of people and you become extremely nervous and stressed. As a result, you forget what you wanted to say. In short, you freeze.

- You're taking an exam, and because you are stressed and under pressure, you are unable to focus your *Mind* and answer the questions.

- You're in the midst of a conversation with someone and the information you want to convey is "*on the tip of your tongue*" but you just aren't able to remember that person's name, that author, that book title or some other information,

- You're driving and suddenly you become aware of a traffic problem ahead of you. By simply placing your thumb and first two fingers together and taking a deep breath, your *Mind* will remain calm, alert and in control so that you can better make the best decision as to what actions you should take.

- You're about to present your business proposal to an important new client or your boss.

- You're in the midst of a '*full on*' disagreement or argument with another person and you desire to remain in control of your reactions, so as not to regret later what you said or how you over-reacted.

Once you start seriously using the **Relaxation Trigger,** you will find many more uses for this technique in your daily life.

Importance of
Stress Management

A long list of health problems that have been directly associated with Stress. Health problems such as: hypertension, heart attacks, strokes, mental & emotional breakdowns, some forms of cancers, to name just a few.

How often does stress interfere with your meals by upsetting your digestion, or even turning you away from the table at minor annoyances, like a child spilling milk? And how much does this lack of proper nourishment in turn affect your health?

Our industrialized, urbanized Western society has become one that requires millions of tranquillizers per year and oceans of alcohol as a means to cope with its stress-filled environment. Some people don't bother with all that; rather they just drift into *a* fantasy world called *"Mental Illness."*

How many people come home, exhausted from a day of stress at work, and just shout at family members to *"Be quiet and let* me *relax?"* There is often a chain reaction that takes place when one works in a highly *'stressed'* environment. A common scenario is: The boss yells at the employee – the employee goes home and yells at the spouse – the spouse yells at the kids – and the kids kick the cat.

FIGHT

WORK

EXCESSIVE
WORK

ORGANISATIONAL
FIGHTING:
MEMOS
MEETINGS
TAKEN HOME:
Spouse
Dog

EXCESSIVE
COMPLAINTS

CONSTANT
Fighting

CAUSING
ACCIDENTS

PHYSICAL
ATTACK

NORMAL

ILLNESS

SLEEP EXCESSIVE:
T.V.
Etc.

HOPELESS
FATALISTIC
WITHDRAWAL

WORK
AVOIDED:
Spend
Time On:
1. Other Interests
2. Out of Town

QUIT
TRYING

PLATEAU OUT

HAVING
ACCIDENTS

PHYSICAL,
IMMOBILISATION

FLIGHT

*Stress is a normal and natural aspect of life. However, without learning to manage your stress it will ulti-
mately lead to a breakdown in relationships, whether personal or work-related, as well as becoming a major health factor. Excessive stress has been linked to heart problems, strokes, breakdown of the immune
system, to death itself. Stress Management is one of the fundamental and most vital skills
that needs to be learned and mastered.*

In addition, for many people, the only way they can overcome stress in order to get a full night's sleep is with the aid of sleeping pills and barbiturates. Unfortunately, such medications tend to interfere with the normal sleep cycles and leaves the person so tired and exhausted in the morning, that they need amphetamines or *'Uppers'* just to get themselves going again.

Scores of headache remedies are advertised to help people get rid of tension-induced headaches – headaches that they could have rid themselves of naturally – if they only knew how. (By the way, you will know how to *Eliminate Headaches,* as the technique is included in the toolbox.)

How often have you developed *"mental blocks"* when put under stress and pressure? And how much has this hampered your creativity, your productivity and your overall job performance?

How many habits and activities - like cigarette smoking, drinking, over-eating and even sex - are things that are used to burn off the immediate torture of the stress that builds up in one's life?

And how much has stress, which comes with one or more of the mentioned problems, undermined your self-confidence and your self-image?

As detrimental as excessive stress can be, most people have little or no understanding of the nature of stress and its relationship to the *Quality of Their Lives.* To help you gain *a* better understanding of stress and the possible impact it may be having on your life, take the following *"Stress Test"* and find out,

----

Stress Test

T. F. Stress in one's own life is harmful and should be eliminated. _____

T. F. Stress and distress mean the same thing. _____

T. F. The food you eat can cause stress. _____

T. F. You are responsible for the stress you experience. _____

T. F. Your health is related to the amount of stress you experience.

T. F. Air and water can be stressful. _____

T. F. Other people are responsible for most of your stress. _____

T. F. Modern drugs are the most effective means of reducing or controlling stress. _____

T. F. One knows when one is under stress. _____

T. F. One can learn to cope with stress but not control stress. _____

Stress Test Answers

1) Stress in one's own life is harmful and should be eliminated.

No, not necessarily. Stress in itself is a normal and natural aspect of everyday life. Perhaps the only time we will be free of stress is when we are *"dead"* -- so as long as you intend to be alive, expect some stress. Further, anything that causes *"change"* causes stress. This is regardless of what may be causing the *"change."* Take for example, exercise, jogging, dancing, a special event (getting married, packing for your holiday, etc.) all cause stress. So being stressed is not, in and of itself, bad. The problem arises when a person becomes overwhelmed with stress and is unable to manage or neutralize it properly before it causes any harm.

2) Stress and distress mean the same thing.

No. Stress, as defined above, is a normal factor of life. Usually, most people have the ability to cope with a certain amount of stress before it becomes detrimental to their health and well-being. There are actually two types of stress 1) *Eustress* and 2) *Distress*. *Eustress* is often known as a *'positive stress'* which is necessary for a person to reach maximum performance in his/her life. Distress is just the opposite; it can be extremely harmful to you on both physically and mentally.

Eustress could be said to be a desirable form of *'Stress'* and is actually healthy for you. Some examples of *Eustress* are: Physical Exercising, Dancing, Amusement Rides (i.e. roller-coasters), etc. if, and this is important, the person enjoys it. If the stress that a person experiences is *perceived as undesirable,* it becomes *'Distress'* for that person. As an example: physical exercise has been found to be excellent source of *'Eustress' for those who enjoy exercising.* Yet, for those who don't enjoy exercising, it is a source of *'Distress.'* Sorry for the cliché but *"One person's wine is another person's vinegar."*

Regardless, what needs to be remembered is that *'distress'* is the culprit and must be neutralized and controlled to prevent it from causing any damage, physically or mentally. Perhaps though, one of the easiest and quickest ways to neutralize stress/distress is through relaxing the body and *Mind* via guided relaxation, such as what *"The Relaxation Training Exercise"* provides.

1) The food you eat can cause stress.

Definitely Yes, Certain foods, by their nature, will cause the body to become highly stimulated, which in turn is placing additional stress on the body. Consuming large amounts of *'caffeine', 'high-fat foods'* and other foods that stimulate or cause the body difficulty in digesting it, can definitely cause unnecessary stress to you both physically and mentally.

2) You are responsible for the stress you experience.

Yes and No. By the very fact that you are alive, you will be experiencing stress. You are, however, responsible if you allow the stress to become distress. Therefore, it will be your responsibility to ensure that you regularly exercise and practice your *'Relaxation Exercise'.* In doing so, you will be neutralizing any excessive stress/distress within your body and *Mind.*

3) Your health is related to the amount of stress you experience.

Another definite Yes. Excessive stress/distress has a direct bearing on your health. Whether it is heart attacks, strokes, obesity, as well as, various cancers, ulcers and immune system diseases can have a direct relationship with the amount of stress/distress a person experiences in his/her life. *Stress Management* is one of the best preventive ways to ensure that excessive stress/distress does not create preventable health problems.

4) Air and water can be stressful.

Yes. Pollutants in both air and water definitely cause your body to be stressed. Therefore, ensuring that the air you breathe (living in a clean environment or use an air purifier) and the water you drink (drinking filtered or bottled water whenever possible) will definitely lessen a significant amount of stress that air and water can produce.

5) Other people are responsible for most of your stress.

No. Even though other people can act and behave in ways that might irritate, frustrate or upset you, they will always remain the stimulus. You, however, can learn to control how you react/respond to what they say and what they might do.

6) Modern drugs are the most effective means of reducing or controlling stress.

No. Relaxants, such as Valium and the like, can help a person, who for a variety of reasons, may be unable to manage the stress in his/her own life. Unfortunately, most, if not all Relaxants can have significant side effects, including addiction. Learning to control the stress of day-to-day life by mastering 'The *Relaxation Technique*' would allow a person to manage the stress naturally, without any of the side effects normally associated with nearly all Relaxants on the market. If your doctor has recommended that you use Relaxants, you might want to talk to your doctor about the possibility of using '*Relaxation*' rather than taking the medication.

7) One knows when one is under excessive stress.

Not Necessarily. That is one reason why '*Stress*' has been referred to as a '*silent killer.*' This is especially true for those individuals who are, by their nature, highly strung, compulsive and believe that they need to work under stress in order to be successful. If one is under stress for a significant period of time, an individual tends to accept such *stress-feelings* as '*normal.*' In our years of teaching, we have had countless people tell us that they never knew they were so '*high strung*' and '*stressed*' until they learned how to relax naturally.

8) One can learn to cope with stress but not control stress.

True. Some individuals live and work in a high-pressure, highly stressed environment. Sometimes the people one lives with and work with are constantly creating a stressful environment. In such cases, one may not be in a position to control the source of the stress (namely those individuals) but one is always in a position to prevent that stress from being internalized within oneself. So if you are in such a situation, whether at home or at work, it's all the more essential that you take charge of your life and practice *Stress Management* on a daily and serious basis -- your health, happiness and the quality of your life depends upon you doing so.

So the case against excessive stress is strong and the case for listening to *"The Relaxation Exercise Training"* becomes even stronger. We simply cannot emphasize enough how important it is for you to master *Relaxation* in your life. Knowing what you know now about the need to relax and control excessive stress in your life might convince you to *"Relax"* on a daily basis ... for the rest of your life.

The Quality Sleep Technique

Obtaining a *'Good Night's Sleep'* is essential for everyone's health and well-being. So even though you may not feel you have a problem sleeping, using this technique will ensure that the sleep you are getting will be sufficient but also of the best quality. Besides, by reinforcing and embedding this technique for a mere 14 nights, you will be guaranteeing that you will be able to fall asleep easily whenever you desire and sleep well regardless of problems, concerns and stress that you might be experiencing. With practice, it will require less than a minute or two to use when you're ready to go to sleep. Considering the numerous benefits you will receive it will definitely be time well spent.

Everyone has experienced those periodic sleepless nights when it is difficult or impossible to sleep. Unfortunately those restless and/ or sleepless nights are a far too common experience for far too many people. As we all know, without a good night's sleep everything you do the next day is tainted. When you are tired and exhausted, you find it hard to not only concentrate, think clearly and to make good decisions but you find it difficult to even enjoy the nice things, such as being with your best friends, eating a good meal, or even making love with the person you adore. The fact is, you simply need your sleep and there's no way around that (except using drugs, and they will only increase your problems in the long run, rather than solve them).

Isn't it somewhat surprising that nature has set aside nearly 1/3 of your life for sleeping. To truly appreciate how significant that is, let's imagine that you live to be 90 years old, nearly 30 years of your entire life would have been spent sleeping. 30 years! Now, if you are not getting the maximum benefit from these numerous years of sleep, you are in fact wasting 30 years of your life. But in addition to that, the quality of the 60 years that you will be awake will have been severely compromised. Sleep on that, if you will.

What Causes Poor Sleeping Habits?

There are many reasons why a person might develop *"poor sleeping habits."* It might be due to such things as unmanaged stress and anxiety in their lives (going to sleep worrying about money, relationship problems, etc.), the result of various medications which have been taken for a significant amount of time (perhaps to control severe pain), working split or random shifts on their job (airline personnel, factory workers, firefighters, to name only a few). Regardless of the reason, the need to obtain a normal and natural sleep is vital if one is to maintain and enjoy a life of quality and good health.

Please Note: Even though this technique seems to suggest that it should be used by people who have a problem *"going to sleep"*, it is extremely beneficial for those who have a problem of *"sleeping too much."* Therefore, we strongly recommend that it be used by every reader for at least 14 nights. The reason for this is that it will realign and reinforce your internal *'sleep patterns'* to help ensure that you receive all the benefits that come with obtaining a *"good night's sleep"*,

The Purpose:

The *Quality Sleep Technique* is an all-purpose sleep technique that will help you to:

1. ***Fall* asleep *easily and quickly.***
   For many people, just trying to fall asleep is their major issue. They will get close to the 'drop-off point when inevitably some disruptive thought pops into their *Mind*

and the game is over. That disruptive thought may have triggered some concern, fear or anxiety such as: *"How can I pay my rent by Friday?"* and the *Mind* becomes stressed-out rather than relaxed. The result: instead of feeling sleepy, the person is now lying there totally awake. We've all been there periodically, but for some people this is a nightly event.

2. *Remain asleep until you desire to awaken.*
There are other people who don't have a problem falling asleep but their problem is to remain asleep. When they wake up, they are unable to return to sleep. This type of sleep problem is more prevalent than one would think. Again, The Quality Sleep Technique will usually correct this problem within 2-3 nights.

3. *Reduce the number of hours you need to sleep*
We have received numerous reports from people stating that as a result of using The Quality Sleep Technique, they were requiring significantly less sleep while feeling far more refreshed and revitalized the next morning. Many of our students have reported that their need for sleep was reduced from, let's say, 9-10 hours per night to 6-7 hours, This reduction in the need for sleep is most probably due to the fact that by using the technique, they were realigning their Sleep Patterns. As a result of this realignment, they were obtaining a significantly better quality sleep.

The Technique:

Use this technique when you are actually in bed and ready to go to sleep. For many people, when they are serious about going to sleep, they often have a certain position in which they place themselves when they are finished thinking and reviewing their day and are serious about going to sleep. It is when you are in this pre-sleep position that you should begin applying the technique.

To Begin:

Close your eyes and *Center* yourself using your **Relaxation Technique.** When *Centered* -- apply the following **Quality Sleep Technique.**

Keeping your eyes closed, imagine that you have a large red marker in your hand. Imagine in your *Mind* drawing a large number *100* When you have drawn the number *100* -- imagine erasing the number *100,* and when you have done so, write the word 'sleep' *(s-l-e-e-p)* -- and when you are writing the word 'sleep', tell yourself *"I'm entering a normal, natural, healthy sleep".*

Then write a large number **99.** Then erase the number **99.** When you have erased the number **99** -- write the word 'sleep' *(s-l-e-e-p)* -knowing that when you write the word 'sleep', you will be entering a normal, natural, healthy sleep.

Then write the number **98.** Then erase the number **98** and write the word -- and when you are writing the word 'sleep', know that when you write the word 'sleep', you will be entering a normal, natural, healthy sleep.

Then write the number **97** -- erase the number **97** and write the word -- knowing that when you write the word 'sleep', you will be entering a normal, natural, healthy sleep.

Then write the number **96** -- erase the number **96** and write the word 'sleep' -- knowing that when you write the word 'sleep', you will be entering a normal, natural, healthy sleep.

Continue using the numbers **95-94-93** and so on until you enter *a* normal, healthy sleep.

When you use this technique, be aware that your *Mind* might wander as you are writing the numbers on a descending scale. If you do experience this, gently bring your *Mind* back to writing the numbers until you do drift into a normal and natural and healthy sleep. The fact that your *Mind* does wonder is actually a good indication that you are entering a normal sleep pattern, so don't be concerned.

After you enter sleep using this technique, if you are awaken during the night because of bathroom needs, phone calls or the baby crying, you will not necessarily need to reapply the technique to return to sleep. If however, you '*feel*' or '*believe*' that your sleep was significantly disrupted and that you will need to *re-apply* the technique, then you will. On the other hand, if you '*feel*' or '*believe*' that getting up for bathroom needs or checking on your child is normal and not an issue, *then you don't need to reapply* the technique. Simply said, if you *believe* you need to *reapply* it, you will need to - If you *don't believe* you need to *reapply* it, you won't. Once again, the power of your '*beliefs*,'

Please Note: If you intend to use any other techniques, such as the "*Problem-Solving While Sleeping Technique*," or the "*Problem-Salving / Goal-Setting Technique*," <u>always</u> apply those techniques <u>prior</u> to using the "*The Quality Sleep Technique.*" Otherwise, you will go to sleep before you would have had an opportunity to apply them. This might seem obvious but we thought we should bring it to your attention before you had to discover the obvious on your own.

PROBLEM-SOLVING
WHILE SLEEPING TECHNIQUE

Your *Mind* can and does solve problems while you are asleep; in fact it's one of the important activities that your *Mind* performs when you are sleeping.

In ancient times, dreams were used by those in authority (or by their soothsayers and holy men) to help them make important decisions which they had to confront in their position as Ruler, Emperor or King. Decisions such as: whether or not to go to war, whether they should join forces with a potential adversary, what did they need to do to appease the gods and goddesses to protect them from famine and diseases ravaging their realm, etc.

There are also numerous references found throughout the Bible, in both the New and Old Testaments, to dreams. They were often referred to as *divine visions* or *visitations* that various prophets and others are said to have had during their sleep. Yet we don't have to look to the past to find references for the importance of dreams. Even in today's world, various branches of psychology consider dreams to be a vital and valuable tool for helping individuals understand, cope and correct various problems they are experiencing in their life. In fact, Sigmund Freud, the *"Father of Psychology,"* referred to dreams as "The *Royal Road"* to access the *Mind's* repressed conflicts.

It would follow that this natural tendency of the *Mind* to sort out the *"concerns of the day"* could be put to good advantage in your life.

The *Problem-Solving While Sleeping Technique* has been designed to provide you the means to program your *Mind* to take *"The Royal Road"* and obtain insights, clarity or answers to various problems and concerns that you may have.

To use the Problem-Solving While Sleeping Technique:

Use this technique when you are actually in bed and ready to go to sleep. Then close your eyes and using your *Relaxation Technique, Center* yourself by relaxing your body and *Mind. When you feel you are Centered,* **say to yourself mentally:**

"I have a problem, which is ... (state the problem clearly and concisely to yourself), and I desire an ideal solution to this problem. I will have this ideal solution and I will easily remember it and understand it in the morning ... and this is the truth"

Then go to sleep from this relaxed level. You may then use the *"Quality Sleep Technique,"* if you so desire. By programming your *Mind* in this manner, you will have a dream that will provide you with your desired *Ideal Solution* to the problem you have been concerned with.

Important to Note: Due to various factors that can influence your sleep cycles, such as tension and stress that you are experiencing, how tired and exhausted you are and/or if your sleep cycle is disturbed because of some unexpected event (a phone call in the middle of the night, your child crying, etc.), may modify the amount of time required for you to arrive at your *Ideal Solution.* So don't be concerned if your *Ideal Solution* does not become apparent after the first night you request it. It may require two to three nights to obtain your *Ideal Solution.* Rest assured however, you will have your *Ideal Solution* and it will be the right one for you.

If however, you do not receive the information you desire within 3 nights, we recommended that you **1)** *"rethink the nature"* of your problem and **2)** ensure that you are not *'secretly'* holding some preconceived *answer* as to what you want the *Ideal Solution* to be. **3)** If necessary, re-word the problem so that it better reflects the true nature of your concern and your true desire.

1 The Interpretation of Dreams by Sigmund Freud - James Strachey - Publisher Basic Books. Place of Publication: New York. Publication Year: 1955

Eliminating Headaches

This technique is a *"Pain Control Technique"* specifically designed to eliminate stress and migraine headaches. We are making an assumption that if you use this technique, it's because you already "know" what type of headaches you are experiencing. We are emphasizing this point because all pain, including headache pain, is your body indicating that something is wrong. As a result, - **DO NOT** - apply this technique to eliminate your headaches until you have a seen your doctor (or medical professional) to determine the exact nature of your headaches. Remember, this technique and all of the techniques we are providing are meant to help you solve problems ... not to create them!

Technique for Eliminating Headaches:

Center yourself and ensure that you are feeling relaxed both mentally and physically. The need to feel relaxed becomes more significant if one is attempting to control pain. The reason for this is, by the nature of pain, it can act as a barrier to achieving an ideal state of relaxation. Therefore, if the pain you are experiencing from the headache seems to be preventing you from relaxing, our experience has shown that it will be helpful for you to break through your *"pain barrier"* by introducing a few *"10-1 countdowns."* That is, simply begin counting from 10-1 slowly, telling yourself that you are "feeling more relaxed with each descending number." Then, when you do feel sufficiently relaxed, apply the Headache Technique.

For Stress/Tension Headaches:

Say to yourself: *"I have a Stress Headache and I do not want to have this headache -- I want to be free from all pain and discomfort that I'm feeling."* Then tell yourself that *"I will count from 1 to 5 and when I reach the count of 5, all of the pain and discomfort that I am feeling will be totally gone."*

Then count slowly from 1 to 3, when you reach the count of 3, again say to yourself *"When I reach the count of 5, all of the pain and discomfort that I'm feeling will be gone."* Then count to 4 and then to 5 -- and at the count of 5, open your eyes and say to yourself, *"I have no pain or any discomfort in my head ... and this is the truth."*

For Migraine Headaches:

It is recommended that you use the following technique *2 or 3 times - 5-10 minutes apart.* The reason for using the technique 2 to 3 times is due to the fact that *Migraine Headaches* tend to involve more than pain and discomfort in the head area. They usually produce an additional range of symptoms, such as: hypersensitivity to light and noise, upset stomach/nausea, etc.

Say to yourself: *"I have a Migraine Headache and I do not want to have this Migraine Headache -- I want to be free from all pain and discomfort that I'm feeling."* Then tell yourself that *"I will count from 1 to 5 and when I reach the count of 5, all of the pain and discomfort that I am feeling will be totally gone."*

Then count slowly from 1 to 3, when you reach the count of 3, again say to yourself *"When I reach the count of 5, all of the pain and discomfort that I'm feeling will be gone."* Then count to 4 and then to 5 -- and at the count of 5, open your eyes and say to yourself, *"I have no pain or any discomfort from my Migraine Headache ... and this is the truth."*

IMPORTANT: When you have finished the Headache Technique, whether for *Stress/Tension Headaches* or for *Migraine-type Headaches*, <u>do not question the results</u> from the technique. Rather just get on with the business at hand. The reason for this is that, if you begin to check for whether the pain, discomfort and symptoms have been eliminated, you are in fact *"questioning"* the effectiveness of the technique, which will affirm your *"disbelief"* that the technique works. Remember, we are dealing with actual physiological pain, and as a result, the body will often require some additional time (perhaps a few minutes) to actually neutralize and eliminate the pain, discomfort and symptoms that you were experiencing. The important thing is that your headache will be gone.

IMPROVING MEMORY & RECALL:

We are sure you do not have to be convinced of the importance of having the ability to memorize and recall information easily and quickly. The *"Improving Memory & Recall Technique"* has been specifically designed to help you to easily memorize and recall information you have read or have heard.

The *"Improving* Memory & *Recall Technique"* is simply expanding the usefulness of an already embedded technique, *The Relaxation Trigger*. As the *Subconscious Mind* is the seat of your general memory and *The Relaxation Trigger* allows you to reach your *Subconscious Mind*, this technique will greatly enhance your ability to memorize and recall information quickly and easily.

The *"Improving Memory & Recall Technique"* can be incredibly useful and beneficial whenever you want to memorize and recall information, such as:

When Listening to Another Person or Lecturer:

Prior to the start of the meeting, class or lecture, close your eyes and *Center* yourself. Closing your eyes while waiting for the meeting, class or lecture to begin can be usually be done without necessarily drawing attention to yourself. Then, with your eyes closed, use your *Relaxation Trigger* by simply placing your thumb and first two fingers together. Keeping your eyes closed, takes 3 deep breaths in order to achieve a mild state of physical and mental relaxation. When you feel you have achieved this mild state of relaxation, **say to yourself:**

"The information that I hear at this the meeting (class or lecture), I will be able to recall easily and quickly, at any time in the future, with the use of the 'Relaxation Trigger.' And this is the truth."

Then open your eyes and, keeping your fingers together, begin listening to whoever is presenting the meeting, class or lecture:

PLEASE NOTE: If during the meeting, class or lecture your concentration falters and/or your *Mind* starts to wander, simply reapply the *Relaxation Trigger* by putting your fingers together and take a deep breath.

When the meeting, class or lecture is finished, simply get up and leave. There is no need for any additional programming as all required programming was done before hand.

When Reading any Book, Report, or Article:

Whenever you are about to read any information that you want to be well embedded in your *Subconscious* for easy recall later, close your eyes and *Center* yourself prior to reading the material. When you feel you are *Centered* and relaxed, **say to yourself:**

"I will be able to recall, quickly and easily, all information that I will read - at any time in the future with the use of the 'Relaxation Trigger.' And this is the truth."

Then open your eyes and keeping your fingers together, begin reading the material.

PLEASE NOTE: If while reading, your concentration falters and/or your *Mind* starts to wanders, simply reapply the *Relaxation Trigger* by putting your fingers together and take a deep breath.

When you are finished reading the material, there is no need for any additional programming, as all required programming was done before hand.

How to Recall the Information You Had Heard or Read:

You can use the *Relaxation Trigger* to recall <u>any</u> information better, regardless of whether that information was actually programmed with the above techniques or not. The reason is that the *Relaxation Trigger Technique* has as its primary purpose to help you enter your *Subconscious Mind* quickly and easily. Therefore, using the *Relaxation Trigger* will greatly enhance your recall of any information that is stored within your *Subconscious*. Of course, if the information you desire to recall had been programmed to be recalled with the *Relaxation Trigger,* your ability to recall that information will be greatly enhanced.

Recalling Any Information With the Use of the Relaxation Trigger:

Whenever you desire to recall any of the information that you have programmed, simply use the *Relaxation Trigger,* take a deep breath (or breaths) and allow your *Mind* to relax. Then say, "*The information that I require will come to me in a moment.*" It's important that you remain relaxed and don't struggle to try and remember the information you desire. The information will come to you if you give your *Mind* the chance to find it and bring it to your attention.

A modified version of using the Relaxation Trigger to recall information is essentially the same except you can use it in everyday conversations. As an example, imagine you are friends and you want to share with them some information, whether it be a person's name, a book title, the name of a certain restaurant, etc. However suddenly your Mind "goes blank." <u>*Don't struggle*</u> to remember the information you desire but rather discreetly use the *Relaxation Trigger* and saying to your friends, "*It'll come to me in a moment*" and then drop any concern or attempt to recall that information -- if you don't, your stress to remember that information will only increase your problem to remember it. Rather carry on with the conversation you were having with your friends. Then suddenly, for no apparent reason, the desired information "*just pops into your Mind.*"

Once again, this is so important ... if you do start struggling or becoming tense in your effort to recall any information, your *Mind,* due to the tension, will begin shifting to a higher brain frequency. As it moves to the higher brain frequencies, it will be moving further away from the *Subconscious Level,* the very level where the information is located ... So stay relax!

If You Are At a Meeting or In a Classroom Situation:

If your supervisor or professor calls on you to answer a question, use your *Relaxation Trigger* (which can easily be used discreetly without anyone noticing). Before you start to answer, take an easy, deep breath, and while exhaling consciously think to yourself *"Relax"* (and mean it) -- then gather your thoughts and begin to answer the question. Initially you may think that an extremely long and inappropriate amount of time has passed before you begin to answer the question. In fact, it will most probably be no more than *a* few seconds to achieve this ideal state of mental relaxation that will enhance your recall of information you desire. We're serious!

If You Are Taking a Test or Exam:

If your *Mind* goes blank or you are unable to answer a question on a test/exam, close your eyes and use The *Relaxation Trigger*. Once you feel you are *Relaxed* and *Centered*, ask yourself again the question that you were unable to answer and say to yourself *"I know the answer to this question and it will* come *to me in a moment."* It's important that you then clear your *Mind* and stay relaxed in order to allow the required information to come to you. When you have your information, open your eyes and write down the information that came to *Mind*.

If *"nothing"* comes to *Mind,* open your eyes but remain relaxed and move on to the next question. The information you require will most probably surface as you continue answering the other questions.

This often happens due to the fact that your initial attempts most probably caused your *Mind* to *"tense up"* rather than to *"loosen up."* So stay Relaxed ... as it's the key to remembering information! Remember that!

If You Are Writing Essays or Reports:

If you are writing a report and you are not sure as to what to write or your *Mind* simply goes blank, close your eyes and *Center* yourself. Once you feel your *Mind* is relaxed, start thinking about what you should write in a relaxed, calm manner. When you are ready, open your eyes and calmly start writing/typing the information that comes to your *Mind*. If nothing comes to *Mind*, remain relaxed and do something else, such as reviewing what you have already written or taking a short break. The information you require will most probably surface as you redirect your *Mind*. Remember; stay relaxed to help your *Mind* "*loosen up*" rather than "*tense up*."

UNDERSTANDING
PROBLEM SOLVING & GOAL-SETTING

Before the techniques for *Problem Solving and Goal Setting* are introduced, we need to explore in depth, the nature of and the principles behind these two important aspects of your lives.

As an adult, a significant amount of your day-to-day thinking most probably is in some way or other, directly or indirectly involved in *Problem Solving* or some form of *Goal Setting*. Are you not constantly thinking about: *'What you need to do and how to do it'*, *'What you want and how to get it'*, *'How you want things to be'*, *'How will I get her/him to go out with me?'*, *'How do I overcome this health problem?'*, *'Should I buy that new* car?', etc. etc. -- a never-ending to-do list.

Unfortunately, this *'never-ending'* list of problems usually results in living a life that becomes a *'never-ending'* battle with stress, tension and endless worrying. You find yourself hoping and praying that you will find a way to solve these problems ... and be free of them forever. If your prayers are answered and you find ways to get what you want, you perhaps might feel how *'lucky'* you were. If on the other hand, you don't get what you want and your problems persist, you might console yourself by thinking "*Well, that's life*". Fortunately, that's not *'Life'* or at least it doesn't need to be!

If your life has been a *'never-ending'* battle of problems and conflicts, you may have understandably come to believe that, "*you win some, you lose some and there's nothing you can do about it ... that's just the way life is."* If this has become your belief about the way life is, then we have some very good news for you ... just read on.

Your Success Instinct:

Instinct: n.
a natural or inherent-aptitude, *impulse,* or *capacity*

a: *a largely inheritable and unalterable tendency of an organism to make a complex and specific response to environmental stimuli without involving reason.* ***b:*** *behavior that is mediated by reactions below the conscious level.*

Did you know that you were born with a *"Success Instinct"*? This instinct is *'meant for you to succeed in getting what you want.'* Seriously! If you think we are making this up, just observe a newborn baby. A baby will *'naturally'* and *'instinctively'* (without needing to be taught) reach out to get what it wants. You don't have to teach a child to want something, or to demand something, or to reach for and grab what it does want. It's part of the human genetic coding to do so. So, if you have stopped *'reaching for,' 'going for'* and *'grabbing what you want in life',* then something has seriously messed with and reprogrammed your *Subconscious.*

Such a fundamental reprogramming of your *Subconscious* might be the result of you having failed to get what you wanted so many times that various **Disempowering Beliefs** have been created in order to account for and justify your numerous failures and inadequacies. *"I'm just not as good as others.", "I never do anything right.", "I wasn't meant to have that.", "Others probably need it more than I do.", "I really didn't really need that anyhow."* ... blah, blah, blah.

Perhaps, your *Subconscious* has had its natural **Success Instinct** deactivated by the very people who truly loved and cared for you the most. Loved and trusted caretakers, such as your own parents, teachers, religious leaders etc., could have embedded such *Disempowering-Beliefs,* in their sincere desire to protect you from getting hurt and disappointed by the realities of life. Perhaps you were taught that: *"Life* *wasn't meant to be easy."*, *"Don't set your expectations too high as you may get disappointed."*, *"Money is the root of all evil."*, *"If you didn't get it, God didn't want you to have it"* ... and we're sure you have heard these and many other similar *Disempowering Beliefs.*

Regardless of how well-meaning parents and others wanted to be, teaching a child such *Disempowering Beliefs* will never protect that child from future disappointment but rather will most likely guarantee it. *Disempowering Beliefs* will, by their nature, override that child's natural *Success Instinct* to achieve the best that life can offer. It's ironic that many parents, who truly dedicate their lives to ensure that their children receive the best education, in the hopes that they will be successful in life, will often prevent their children's future success by instilling in them such *Disempowering Beliefs.* So ironic and so unfortunate, isn't it? If they only knew.

So as you proceed, be aware that initially you might find yourself having to confront some *Disempowering Beliefs* from your past. As a result, you might find yourself feeling somewhat reluctant and uncomfortable in:

1. Programming to find a *Solution* to a specific problem in your life because you have a belief that perhaps you *"deserve"* to have such a problem
2. Programming for some significant *Goal* because you have a belief that perhaps *"You don't deserve having what you're asking for."*

If you do discover that you have such *Disempowering Beliefs* from your past that are lurking behind the scenes, don't worry. We assure you that if you persist in your programming, you will learn to *deactivate them* and *reactivate* your natural *'Success Instinct.'* Then, when reactivated, you will instinctively find yourself once again *'reaching for'*, *'going for'* and *'getting what you want in life'*.

We strongly urge you to take the time to study the following rules carefully to ensure that you achieve your goals and achieve them quickly.

The Rules Governing Problem-Solving & Goal-Setting:

Techniques such as those for *"Quality Sleep"* and *"Improved Memory"* are, for the most part, self-contained. By 'self-contained', we mean that these techniques deal exclusively with you and only you. No one else is or needs to be involved. On the other hand, the techniques of *Problem Solving* and *Goal Setting* often involve others. If you desire to solve a problem in your relationship with your spouse, it's obvious that your spouse's feelings, actions and behavior will be extremely important, not just yours. In the same way, if you desire to be promoted in your job, your supervisor's feelings, actions and behavior will need to be taken into consideration, if you are to achieve your goal. As a result, the dynamics of the *Problem Solving & Goal Setting Technique* play by somewhat different rules and it is these rules that we now will focus on.

Rule 1:
Never use the power of your Mind to make an 'Intolerable' situation 'Tolerable.'

An example of doing just that would be if the relationship you are in is one where you feel humiliated, abused and/or mistreated. You may be tempted to program yourself that you will become tolerant and accepting of that situation. *No, no and again no!*

Rather, begin programming that the relationship you are in will change and that you will no longer be humiliated, abused and/or mistreated by the other person. Program that you will feel loved, cared for and respected in that relationship. Be aware though, the *solution* might be that you might need to leave that relationship you are in because the other person in the relationship is simply unwilling or unable to change. As undesirable as that solution might seem to be, it may be the only way to give both of you a chance to once again be happy. Both of you deserve that. So once again, *never, but never* program to make an *"Intolerable Situation, Tolerable"* ... promise yourself that!

To get an even better understanding of this **Rule 1**, study **Rule 2:**

Rule 2:
You Can Not Control Another Person

As powerful as your Mind is, you cannot, repeat, you cannot control any other person's thoughts, feelings or behavior. Rather, the most you can do is become a significant influence in the way another person thinks, feels and behaves.

As strongly as you might want another person to fall in love with you, that person cannot be forced to do so. Sorry about that! Don't blame us; blame that person's *'Free Will'*. Individuals will always retain their ability to *"accept* or reject" any thoughts, desires or actions you send their way. So regardless of how powerful you might think you are, you can never, but never, force another person *'to love you'*, 'to care *about you'* or 'to *fulfill* you' -- unless that person chooses to do so. A jealous husband can lock his wife away from the world but he can never unlock her heart. And thank God for that! If in any way you are disappointed by this reality, just remember ... if you could actually control the thoughts and feelings of another person, there's no reason why others couldn't control yours ... then good-bye to *'Free Will.'*

Further, there are enough attempts being made to control other peoples' thoughts and behavior through 'guilt', 'fear', political imprisonment, etc. So if your goal is to force someone to change or do what you want, forget it!

Don't give up hope though. Just because you cannot control someone, doesn't mean you can't program to be in a caring, loving relationship. If you begin programming to be in a loving relationship, your *Subconscious Mind* will start doing whatever is necessary to make that happen.

Since it cannot control anyone but you, your *Subconscious* might instead begin to change your thoughts, feelings and behavior, in its attempt to make you more desirable to the other person. This can result in you: saying and doing things differently so that you become more 'attractive' to the other person. You might find yourself saying things in a better way, or choosing not to say something you were ready to say. You might find yourself deciding to dress differently, feeling it would be more appropriate. You might find yourself becoming m o re 'gently assertive' or 'less pushy' – 'more talkative' or 'more quiet and reserved'

... whatever. The point is, don't be surprised if you start finding subtle changes taking place in your own thoughts, feelings and behavior. And for goodness sake, allow these changes to take place. Remember, they are being initiated by your own Subconscious in its attempt to get you what you want.

Remember that your *Subconscious* must work in your best interest and it has the best understanding of what would be required to give you what you want. So trust it. As you are working with your *Subconscious*, don't get impatient and remain alert to any new situation, opportunity or feedback that might arise. They can be quite subtle, by the way. It may be a look, a glance, a touch, a smile, a word or words, some unexpected warm reply or response, etc. that might provide you the needed feedback that your *Subconscious Programming* is working.

Having said this, there is one thing you must do. You must be absolutely 100% yourself. If in any way you're not being truthful as to whom you really, really are, then if a relationship does develop, that relationship will be between the other person and someone else, who is only pretending to be you. You are then left in a dilemma forever -- you will never be able to be truly yourself but will have to always pretend that you're that other person. Trust us, you'll be found out ... it's not worth it. So just be yourself from the beginning. Besides, if the other person cannot accept you for who you truly are, you'll never truly enjoy being in that relationship anyhow.

This rule, by the way, applies to any situation that involves another person and is not restricted to *Intimate Relationships*. If you're going for a "*job interview*", all of the same principles will apply. Before going for that job interview, seriously program your *Subconscious* to ensure that it will guide your *thoughts*, *words* and *actions* throughout that interview. Be sure to program sufficiently to ensure that your *Subconscious* knows exactly what you want, so that it can do its job properly.

Rule 3:
Program Your 'GOAL' -- Not Your 'SOLUTION'

This third rule is extremely important and very significant. Let's use the same two examples as we did in **Rule 2.**

Programming Relationships:

If your goal is to be in an *'Ideal Relationship'* where you will feel *"love, cared for and fulfilled"*, then program just that, and only that. Don't start dictating to your *Subconscious* who you want as the solution. Even if you might strongly want to have that relationship with a specific person, your first and highest priority is to have *"a relationship that will provide you love, caring and fulfillment."* If that can be achieved with that *"certain somebody"* great! If not, it really won't matter if in the long run, you achieve your ultimate goal of having *"the relationship that you desire."* Right?

Let's look at this point again. If your goal/desire is that you want to be in a loving, caring and fulfilling relationship, your desire is clear, straightforward and achievable.

On the other hand, if your goal is that *"You want a loving, caring and fulfilling relationship with John Buck or Jane Doe"*, you are now programming a specific *Solution*. To achieve this, your *Subconscious* would need to program John or Jane to love, care and fulfill you whether they wanted to or not. And your *Subconscious* is simply powerless to do that. Why? Simple. Remember that John or Jane have *"Free Will."* Your Mind cannot impose its will on another person, unless that person agrees to it. End of story. Therefore, don't waste your time trying to do it! Rather program your most fundamental desire, that of having a loving, caring and fulfilling relationship, and let your *Subconscious* get to work without you imposing limitations or restrictions.

We think a story regarding programming a Relationship is in order:

A student, who was repeating one of Tom's seminars, stood up and shared with the class his story regarding finding his *'Ideal Relationship'*:

He began by saying that after he had attended the seminar the first time, he was determined to find the *"woman of his dreams."* He began to seriously program for a date with a woman he wanted to date for over six months. He programmed that she would agree to not only go out with him but would, in time, agree to marry him. He admitted he was quite obsessed with her. He couldn't get her out of his mind and his obsession prevented him from even considering dating anyone else.

He began to use his *Goal Setting Technique* that he had learned in the Seminar. He diligently programmed for this relationship every day and sometimes twice a day. Within two weeks she actually approached him at work and told him that for some unknown reason, he kept popping into her mind during the past week. She then invited him to a party. Of course he accepted immediately and couldn't believe '*his luck.*'

When they arrived at the party, she began drinking quite heavily and within an hour or so she had reached her limit. She became louder and more boisterous, she began pushing herself on other men at the party, stumbling twice and had to be helped off the floor ... you get the picture. Even though he kept offering to take her home -- she kept telling him to mind his own business and let her have some fun. Finally she just passed out. He, of course, did the right thing and dragged her to his car and proceeded to drive her home. During all this, he kept thinking to himself how the evening was a total disaster and how his "*Goal-Setting Programming*" was totally useless.

But the story doesn't end there ...

The following evening, after he returned home from work, he had a phone call. The person who was calling was the woman whose party he had attended the previous evening. She said she called just to say how much she admired him in regards to how he handled himself the previous evening under such difficult circumstances. She went on to say that it was so refreshing for her to see a man with such integrity. She then asked him if he would like to come to her place to have dinner the following evening.

So, the following evening he was at her door for dinner ... and the rest is history. They were married seven months later. His new wife, with a smile on her face, was sitting next to him in the seminar room as he was telling his/their story.

The point that must be made is that when he was programming for his '*Ideal Relationship*', he was in fact, programming for what he believed was the '*Ideal Solution*' (by programming for a relationship

118

with a specific person). This is important, very important! Program your *Goal* and not what or whom you think is the *Solution*.

Let's try another one. This one will be in regards to programming for a *New Job*

Programming for a New Job or Career:

Initially, when you begin programming to find a *New Job*, your goal should be the things you desire from that a job and not an actual job with a specific company. Otherwise, you will be programming what you think is your solution. Making this distinction is important anytime you are doing any type of job seeking. Simply take the time to determine what you desire and what you need from any job that you would consider accepting. These desires and needs are your Goal.

As an example:

- The minimum amount of money you would consider acceptable

- The number of hours you would be willing to work per week.

- Job perks, such as, travel expenses, domestic and international travel.

- A private office. etc....

It doesn't matter what your requirements are. What is important is that you are very clear as to what you want at your job requirements are. If you start programming that you simply want '*a job*' then be prepared to accept whatever comes your way. By programming for just '*a job*', you are leaving yourself open to get '*some job*' but not necessarily one that will meet your list of personal requirements. If you program for '*a job*', you might get a job offer but it might not be what you were looking for. It could be a job in an all-night diner, needing to work from 1 a.m. to 6 a.m., and paying minimum wages or less per hour. If this happens, don't complain, because that's what you asked for ... '*I want a job*'! Your *Subconscious Mind* did what you asked it to. If you desire to do more than flip hamburgers at 3 a.m., we would suggest that you take the time to clarify precisely as to what type of job you desire and the benefits it will provide you. On the other hand, if you are simply looking for a temporary, part time job to supplement your income, or that type of work you really enjoy, it would be a perfect solution.

Just Remember the Following:

> **"If you're not clear as to what**
> **you want ... be satisfied**
> **with what you get!"**

Programming Your Job in 3 Phases:

Phase 1: Once you have decided precisely as to what you want from a job, begin programming that job. Imagine in your *Mind*, that you have *'a job that meets all of your needs and desires.'* You could imagine yourself sitting in some office that you know is yours (perhaps your name and position is on the door).

You might imagine yourself dictating letters to your secretary. You could also imagine yourself attending business meetings and conferences both domestically and internationally. You could imagine yourself leaning back in your office chair, your hands behind your head, just feeling good, confident and very, very successful.

It's important that you continue programming this image of yourself actually having the job you truly desire. We suggest also that when you are programming this job, to involve as many of your inner senses as possible in your image. Imagine yourself sitting in your *soft and comfortable* office chair (sense of touch) and *opening and closing* your desk drawers (sense of touch and movement). Imagine *eating* (sense of taste & smell) lunch or dinner with the company president or some other top honcho within the company. Even imagine yourself *looking* at your business card, which has your name and job title on it (sense of sight), as well as, any other sensory image that you can create that would indicate that you have actually obtained *'the job you desire.'*

Of course during your initial programming for that job, you will have no idea what company or organization you will be working for

-- but at this stage, you don't need to know. Just keep programming for the job you really would like to have, the details will come later.

As your *Subconscious Mind* is seeking ways to fulfill your needs and desires, it will become *supersensitive* to anything and everything that could possibly help you to obtain the job you desire.

You might be at the party, when suddenly your ears perk up because someone near you is discussing the fact that there is a position that soon will be available in their company. A position that is exactly of the type you are looking for. You're having lunch with friends and you casually drop the fact that you're looking for a new job. Then suddenly, one of your friends says *"Wait a minute, I just spoke with one of my clients today, and he said that he will be leaving his job and the work he was doing happens to be exactly what you are looking for."* You're casually reading the newspaper and your eyes lock onto a small *'Job Ad'* with your future job staring at you. The possibilities are unlimited, so be prepared for your *'Solution'* to make itself known, sometimes in the most unexpected way.

All of this may sound too good to be true. Remember though that when you program your *Subconscious* for something you want, it will become *supersensitive* to anything and everything that could possibly help it to fulfill your needs. It's often uncanny how the needed information you require will come to your attention, sometimes from the most unlikely sources. None of this will ever happen though, unless your *Subconscious* knows precisely what you are asking for. And once your *Subconscious* knows what you want, it has no option but to do whatever is required to help you get what you want.

When Your Subconscious Succeeds in Finding You an "Ideal Job":

Let's say you do become aware of an *'ideal job'* that you would like to apply for. Then kick into action ASAP. Don't even think about postponing, procrastinating or hesitating in applying for that job. Make that phone call and push to get an appointment for that job interview immediately. Then, when your interview has been scheduled, begin *Phase 2* of your *job Hunting* Programming.'

Phase 2: In this phase, you will begin programming the actual interview. Start programming your *Subconscious* by imagining yourself performing at your very best during the interview. Imagine yourself sitting calmly and relaxed while waiting to be called for your interview with the *Personnel Manager*. Then, imagine the interview itself. Imagine yourself responding in a calm, relaxed and confident manner to the questions the *Personnel Manager* is asking. In your *Mind*, create the feeling that the *Personnel Manager* is extremely pleased with the interview and, most of all, with you. Of course you should add to this scene, anything that you personally think might be important if you were actually having this interview. Be sure to imagine yourself remembering to use the **"Relaxation Trigger"** during the interview in order to remain calm, confident and relaxed. Finally imagine that at the end of the interview, the *Personnel Manager* is shaking your hand and telling you that *"He/she thinks you would be ideal for the job and is looking forward to having you work for their company."*

As always, don't get caught up on details. There would be no way for you to know before the job interview what the actual details will be or the sequence of events that could take place when you actually go for the interview. When the actual interview takes place, you might not actually need to sit and wait before being called. Nor would you necessarily be interviewed by the *Personnel Manager*, if they even have one. You might in fact be directed immediately into a small board room, where there is not just one person interviewing you but three. None of this matters except that you remain relaxed and confident and that you present yourself in the best possible way during the interview.

What you are doing and need to do when you are imagining this *"pre-interview"* in your *Mind* is programming your *Subconscious* precisely as to how you want to feel (calm, relaxed and confident) and how you want to be perceived by the interviewer(s) i.e. confident, well spoken, well qualified, etc. Again, don't get caught up on details. Just keep holding that image of yourself obtaining that job. Okay? Good!

Phase 3: After your interview, the thoughts you have regarding that job, will be just as important as the thoughts you had preparing for the interview. It is absolutely vital that you maintain a positive, never wavering belief that you will have that job. Regardless of whether or not you felt the interview went well ... hold *'success'* in your *Mind*. By the way, most people never think that interviews and similar situations, like auditions, ever go as well as they could and should have. Perhaps that's just our human nature and/or our *Subconscious* protecting us from possible disappointment.

Just remember to continue programming that you have that job. Imagine yourself receiving a phone call or letter telling you that *"You Got the Job"*. It's very important that you do not start *worrying* that you didn't. When you worry, you are creating images and thoughts of yourself *'failing or not being successful'*. Think about it -- no one, but no one, ever worries about themselves not succeeding. So if you start *worrying*, you are counteracting and negating your *"Success Instinct"* that you have worked so hard to reactivate in your life. Let nothing sway you from your positive programming until you actually hear something to the contrary regarding that job interview.

Another Story:

This story is from Antonio who had attended one of Elena's seminars. His story, which he shared with the group, is as follows:

Antonio decided to program for a new job. He programmed diligently for a specific type of job and to his delight, he was invited to interview for a job that definitely met most of his needs.

He then programmed the interview before hand. The interview itself went extremely well and exactly as he had imagined. So well in fact, that he was convinced he had the job without any doubt.

However, two days later he received a phone call that informed him that he was not successful in obtaining that job. As devastated as he was, he refused to give up and kept programming for the job he desired.

Then to his surprise, a few days later he received another phone call from that company. The phone call was from the *Personnel Director* he had interviewed with. This person asked Antonio if he could come in for a meeting the following day but he did not explain the reason why. Antonio agreed, even though he had no idea what the meeting would be about. During that meeting, the Personnel Director explained that at the time of the first interview, he was unable, due to company politics, to inform Antonio of an upcoming job that would soon be available. This job, the Personnel Director proceeded to explain, was one that he felt would be better suited for Antonio. The job that was then offered to Antonio was not only of a much higher position within the organization, it would involve international travel and would pay $42,000 more than the job Antonio had originally interviewed for. $42,000 more, not bad! Needless to say, Antonio accepted that job.

The moral of the story -- don't be too eager to assume that your *Goal Setting Programming* hasn't worked. Stay with it and hold firmly within yourself that *"what you want ... you're going to get!"* Your *Subconscious* might just have other plans for you. Besides, it's not over, until it's over.

We are very aware, of course, that Antonio's story is dramatic but we honestly assure you that there are a hundred more we could share that would reflect the same degree of dramatic success through diligent *Goal Setting Programming*. We also assure you that a person like Antonio is no different than you are. He had no additional skills or special mental capabilities than you -- he simply took the principles and the techniques he had learned and really applied them. So why not start applying them in your life – **NOW!**

Programming For Something You Simply Want:

If you want something, whether it's a new car, a trip overseas, a DVD player or any other such item, regardless of how mundane it might be, simply program for what you really *want* and not what you *believe* you can have.

Our experience has been that far too many people program for things that they want based upon what they *believe* they can afford, rather then what they *really want*. The problem with such programming is that it tends not to be successful for a variety of reasons. If you attempt to program for something *"you don't really want"* (because you believe you couldn't afford to have what you really do want), you most probably won't get it due to lack of sincere desire on your part. On the other hand, if you do get it, chances are you will never feel totally satisfied with it, as you didn't get what you really, really wanted. In addition, unfortunately, there is a good chance that you have reinforced in your *Subconscious* a belief that says, *"I never get what I really want.", "I never have enough money"* or any number of other possible *"Disempowering Beliefs."*

Instead, set your goal for what you really want and let your *Mind* figure out how you can get it. Let's say, you would really want a new car. Perhaps your *"Ideal Car"* would be a two-door convertible, with a leather interior, air conditioning, etc. Then program for that car with all of your preferences. As always, be very precise. Even though your finances may be very limited, go for what you want. Never settle for second best. Never compromise.

It's understandable that until you get used to using your *Mind* in this manner, you will tend to make certain assumptions about how you most probably will find the car you want. Unless one is going to steal it, the most obvious way to get the car you want is to go to a Car Dealer or look in the classified ads. We're asking you again to remember that by programming, you are playing by different rules. Of course go to a Car Dealer and take the time looking through the classified ads but allow your Mind to respond to your *'super-sensitive Subconscious.'* The car you so desperately want may already be parked one block away, and just waiting for your *Subconscious* to notice it and the For *Sale Sign* on its window. Chances are your *Subconscious Mind* never took notice of it as it hadn't been programmed to do so. Program for it and you will suddenly begin seeing *'your car'* everywhere. You will see it passing you on the freeway, on billboards, in magazines, etc. -- it will seem as if everyone has the car you want. Therefore, refrain from allowing your *"Logical Mind"* from interfering in the work of your *Subconscious Mind.* Just go for what you want rather than going for something that you believe you could have (due to financial concerns, etc.). Just hold the thought of what you really want, but hold it gently. If you become stressed and obsessed with getting what you want, it indicates *desperation* and not *expectation.* Such desperation usually is the result of having *"doubts"* that your programming will be successful. Continue *'dis-believing'* and it will stop your *Subconscious* from pursuing your goal, as you will be reinforcing a belief that *"you won't get what you want"* rather than believing *"that you will."*

To neutralize such potential doubts and disbeliefs, continue your programming for what you want, with the belief that *'You will have it. How,* you don't know yet but you will have it.'

Case in Point:

A few years ago, Elena relocated from Sydney to Miami for a period of time to establish herself and her seminars in the USA. She was in need of a new car, as the one she was driving she had bought soon after she arrived in the USA and bought it just to get her through the first few months.

Unfortunately the car was reaching the end of *'its road'* a lot sooner than she had anticipated. As the money she had was meant to finance her new seminar business, the sudden need to replace her car was less than ideal timing (which is often the case). Regardless, she refused to let her *'financial reality'* sway her from immediately programming for a new car, one she really wanted and needed.

Even though Elena did not have a specific car in *Mind,* she had decided that a SUV would probably be ideal, as it would provide her sufficient comfort, as well as, sufficient space to transport all of her seminar materials. She admitted later that programming for that new car was initially somewhat of a challenge. Her practical, logical *Mind* kept interfering in her attempts to program her new car. It kept reminding her of her very limited financial resources. Then however, her "*Success Instinct*" kicked in. Essentially a part of her said "*I need a new car, I want a new car and I'm going to have the car I want -- how I'm going to get it, I don't know yet but I will have it.*" And with that shift in her thinking, she seriously began programming for her "*New Car.*"

At least twice a day, Elena took the time to *Center* herself and imagine herself driving her "*brand-new SUV.*" She imagined that even though her SUV was loaded with all of her seminar supplies, there was still ample space available. She imagined herself driving in real comfort, as the SUV had all the extras, from air conditioning to an excellent sound system, etc. She imagined herself driving the SUV in extremely hot Miami weather, yet feelings so cool and comfortable while driving. She imagined herself driving the SUV interstate to visit family and friends and feeling extremely safe and comfortable when doing so.

In addition to programming for her car twice a day, she would always bring to her *Mind* an image of herself *"driving* her *New SUV"* whenever she found herself becoming concerned about the problems she was having with her old car.

Then, about 10 days after she started programming, a Sunday to be exact, she took some time to just stroll through a nearby shopping center. It was on her way back to her car that she noticed numerous flags, balloons and banners in the front of a car dealer. And without consciously deciding to do so, she found herself walking in. She remembers that as she entered, her eyes were immediately drawn to a SUV, in what she thought was an incredibly pleasing metallic blue. Without a chance to even go and look at the car, she was greeted by a Sales Rep. She then explained to him her situation and the type of car that she needed and why. His reply was, *"Today is the last day of our 'Clearance Weekend'* and as we will be closing in the few hours, let's see if we can help you." He then began walking over to the very car Elena had noticed when she walked in. Upon closer look, that car had everything and more than she had been programming for. Of course she looked at a few other cars but nothing seemed to compare with her *'Metallic Blue Sweetheart'* on the showroom floor.

Obviously the Sales Rep noticed her mild obsession and began negotiating with her for the SUV she wanted. After some haggling, they arrived at what she felt was a sensational price, one she knew she could easily afford to pay. When the price was finalized, then came the matter of financing it. Remember, Elena had only been in the country a few weeks or so. She had no credit rating, no credit history, she was *"technically"* unemployed and in addition ... she wasn't in a position to put even $1.00 down of her own money towards the purchase. Yet, without saying a word, the Sales Rep began to make a series of phone calls, even though it was already 8:30 p.m. on a Sunday evening. He then proceeded to walk in to the Manager's Office.

Even though Elena said nothing and seemed to be just waiting. She was in fact, extremely busy mentally. Throughout her wait, she kept holding the images that she had been programming of herself driving *'her Metallic Blue SUV'*, she even saw the SUV's car keys on her keychain.

Then after about 20 minutes, the Sales Rep emerged from the office and said to Elena, *"As I told you, this is our 'Clearance Weekend' and the purpose is to clear as many cars as possible from our lot and inventory. The problem is that you have been in the USA for just a few weeks, we can find no credit history for you and you are unemployed. Normally, we just wouldn't even consider selling a car to a person in your position. However, for some reason I decided to talk to my manager. To my surprise, he has agreed that if you're willing to finance the purchase of the car through our own finance-agent, we could proceed with selling you the car."*

After thinking about it (perhaps for 30 seconds) Elena agreed. She then signed a few forms and said her goodbyes to her beloved, but now nearly dead old car, and drove home in her New Metallic Blue SUV.

In the End She Got:

- The car she wanted.
- At an incredibly good price.
- With monthly payments, well within her means.
- And all the while being technically unemployed.

Does programming work? You be the judge! Magic, we tell you ... it's simply magic!

The above situation emphasizes the importance of being *"precise"* in regards to what you want. As it has been said before ***"If you don't know what you want, be satisfied with what you get."***

Programming for a car, without being precise, leaves you wide open to *"getting a car"* but not necessarily the car you want. Try going to a car dealer and simply tell him that you want *"a car"* and tell him how much money you are willing to pay. Chances are, that car dealer will begin to show you cars that have nothing to do with what you really desire. You might be shown a rusted out 1985 Ford with one wheel missing. Since you were merely programming for *'a car - any car'* then the 1985 Ford, with one wheel missing, meant that you were in fact successful, weren't you? If however, you were programming for a *"SUV"*, with all of your special specifications, as Elena had done, then you weren't. *So be careful what you ask for (or don't ask for), as you most probably will get it.* And always remember ... *'If you want something specific ... be specific'.*

Programming Your Financial Situation:

Be assured that we would be the last one to say that money isn't important ... because it is. Yet, regardless of how useful and necessary money may be, we would strongly suggest that you avoid programming to have *"more money"* in your life.

What we do suggest is that you program for the actual things that you feel will enrich your life and help you live a life of quality. You can be extremely rich but if you are unhealthy, unhappy and unfulfilled, money cannot buy you the health, happiness and self-fulfillment you desire. Like everything else, money in itself, has its limits. So even though a problem you have might seem to require money to help solve it, stay with the formula of programming *'what you want'* rather than *'what you believe is the solution'* which for most people is more money.

Here is an example: Let's say that you have a problem, your rent is due in two week and you do not have the money to pay the rent. Start programming by relaxing and *Centering* yourself. When you feel you are *Centered,* begin imagining in your *Mind* that you are actually *"writing a check for the rent"* or *"giving cash to the landlord"* or however you normally pay your rent. Remember to involve as many of your inner-senses as possible when you are programming. Perhaps you could:

- Imagine feeling the pen between your fingers as you write the check

- Because the payment is due in one week, imagine seeing yourself dating the check before the due date

- Imagine making the check payable to your landlord

- Imagine yourself signing that check

- Imagine yourself placing that check in an envelope, sealing it (and even tasting the glue as you moisten it)

- Imagine yourself addressing the envelope and mailing it

- Then imagine receiving a receipt for your rent payment which will indicate that your rent money was received and your rent is paid.

Create in your Mind a *'Rent-Paying Mini-Movie'* that is as real and as detailed as you can make it. By making it real and in great detail, you are providing your *Subconscious* with the guidelines or script of precisely what you want. Remember though, as concerned as you are about not being able to pay it, you must program your *'Rent-Paying Mini-Movie'* in a calm, confident and relaxed manner. If you begin programming with a feeling of anxiety and/or desperation, you will negate the *'positive belief'* which is absolutely necessary for your mini-movie to become a reality. In other words, you'll be setting yourself up to fail.

After you have completed your programming of your *'Rent-Paying Mini-Movie'*, it will be necessary for you to continue to maintain a *'positive belief/attitude'* that your rent will be paid on time. Do not allow your logical *Conscious Mind* to negate the work you are doing with your *Subconscious*, be assured an answer which will provide an appropriate solution to your problem will become apparent. Perhaps the solution will become apparent during the day, as a flash of insight or while you are sleeping, as a dream. And until that solution becomes apparent, continue to calmly reinforce your *mini-movie* once or twice a day.

After you have succeeded in arriving at the appropriate solution as to how you will pay the rent, we would strangely suggest that you ask yourself *"has paying your rent on time been an ongoing problem in your life?"* If the answer is _yes_, then begin programming yourself to solve the real problem in your life, which in this case, is your tendency to have difficulty meeting your financial obligations.

Start programming yourself by imagining a *mini-movie* that shows you financially comfortable and having overcome the tight, financial situation that you have a tendency of finding yourself in. Perhaps you could imagine your bank statement indicating that you have more than a sufficient amount to pay your rent and the other debts that you have. Imagine yourself depositing significant amounts of money into *"your savings account"*, and doing so on a regular basis. In short, start programming yourself to become a *"financially responsible"* person. However, and this is very important, don't forget to also imagine yourself having nice things and doing enjoyable things (eating out with friends, traveling, etc.) to indicate that you are also able to enjoy your money and not just able to meet your financial obligations. Being a *"financially responsible"* person does not in any way restrict you from spending and enjoying the money you have -- it just means that you do it wisely.

It's only when you start affirming that *"Enough Is Enough, I no longer 'desire' to live on the edge financially"* that you will truly start becoming financially comfortable. As we're sure you know, it's no fun living on the edge, so stop doing it, if you are. Begin by changing your thinking and changing your beliefs about money and your worthiness to have it in your life. Then start doing some serious *Prosperity Programming*.

When *Solutions* begin to surface from your *Subconscious*, starting acting on them in your life. Solutions such as the need for you to:

1. Learn to budget your money better

2. Discipline yourself to say 'no' when you want to buy something that you really don't need

3. Look for opportunities to supplement your income, including finding part-time work or a new full-time job that pays more, etc.

4. Then follow through and do them.

Remember, if you don't change and do things differently, you most probably will be seeking solutions as to how you will pay your bills again next month and probably every month after that. Don't do that to yourself, you deserve so much better...

Programming Your Health:

Even though your body is programmed for self-healing and it will do the best that it can to restore itself to good health, this does not mean you should avoid seeking *Professional Medical help and attention* when serious health problems exists.

Therefore, **DO NOT** use this technique to attempt correcting or healing any serious health problem until you have a seen your doctor or medical professional. Remember, your *Mind* is meant to solve problems and not to create them!

Having made our point, the following will be various examples as to how to apply the power of the *Mind, when it's appropriate to do so,* to eliminate pain and heal the body when necessary.

Eliminating Pain & Severe Discomfort:

When you are experiencing muscle pain from the common flu to arthritis, *Center* yourself and focus on the part of the body in which you are experiencing pain. Create a *mini-movie* in your *Mind* imagining the problem area of your body and imagining the *pain/discomfort* in that area as perhaps a *dark cloud* or *mist*. Then imagine that this *dark cloud* or *mist* is leaving your body through the pores in your skin. Continue with this imagery until the pain subsides and/or is eliminated. Depending on the severity of the pain and discomfort, repeat this *"mini-movie"* as required.

NOTE: If the pain is a result of a serious accident, you can use this technique to significantly reduce the pain until you are able to seek Medical help. Remember, all pain is an indication that something is wrong (sometimes seriously wrong), therefore, do not eliminate the pain without also eliminating the *'cause'* of the pain.

Cuts and Wounds:

Again, if you have experienced any cuts or wounds (including burn wounds), create a *"mini-movie"* while you are relaxed and *Centered*. Imagine that the cut or wound remains pain-free and imagine the cut or wound healing quickly and without any scarring. Depending on the severity of the injury, it is recommended that you reinforce your *"healing-mini-movie"* at least once or twice a day.

Surgery:

As soon as you become aware that you will be entering a hospital and undergoing surgery, for whatever reason, it is highly recommended that you create a *"Surgery Mini-Movie"* of yourself going through and recovering from that surgery. Include in your *"Surgery Mini-Movie"* the following:

1. Imagine yourself prior to surgery remaining calm and relaxed, as well as imagining remaining calm and relaxed throughout the surgery, as this will tend to reduce the production of adrenaline, which can encourage excessive bleeding

2. Then imagine returning to your hospital room and resting comfortably without pain or discomfort.

3. Imagine being told by your doctor(s) how totally successful the surgery was and how well you are recovering.

4. Imagine yourself recovering quickly in the hospital and returning home in a very short period of time -feeling great and in perfect health.

5. Imagine yourself returning to any activities that you may have been prevented from doing due to your health problem or illness.

When You are Actually in the Hospital Waiting for the Surgery:

Continue to mentally play your *"Surgery Mini-Movie"* as often as possible. Play your *"mini-movie"* even as you are being taken into the surgery room. But whatever you do, and this is extremely important, keep playing your *"mini-movie"* in your *Mind* as you are actually being anesthetized! By doing so, your *"mini-movie"*, with its images of quick recovery, will be your last thought prior to your *Mind* drifting into *Unconsciousness*. And as your *Mind* begins to drift, it will carry with it, your *"Healing/Recovery Program"* and embed it deeply into your *Unconscious Realm*.

During Your Recovery:

Following the surgery and throughout your recovery, continue to play your *"mini-movie"* to reinforce your recovery and your quick return to living a *'Life of Quality and Good Health.'*

Colds, Flu and Other Minor Health Problems:

If you find yourself experiencing the symptoms associated with the *'Common Cold, Flu, etc.'*, create a *"mini-movie"* of your body free of the symptoms you are experiencing, i.e. stuffy nose, coughing, fever, muscle aches and pains, etc. Then play this *"mini-movie"* every few hours *(as you would normally do when taking any cold medication)*. Your *"mini-movie"* will play a significant role in helping you recover your good health quickly and easily.

In your *"mini-movie"* you could imagine that you are able to breathe easily, that your lungs are free of any congestion and that you have no desire to cough, etc. You could also imagine taking your temperature and seeing that it is normal. Remember to create and play this *"mini-movie"* as soon as the first symptoms of your *'cold/flu'* appear, and play it frequently.

The sooner you attack your symptoms, the better. So whether you are at work or at home, as soon as you begin to have that thought of *"Damn ... I think I'm coming down with something."* -- get *Centered*, and supercharge your immune system by creating your *"mini-movie"* of good health. It'll only take you a few minutes to do, yet you can save yourself days of feeling miserable.

Start thinking differently about your health -- as nobody's is throwing you *'a cold or the flu'*, there is no need for you to *'catch it.'*

Please Note: If you do use and reinforce your *"mini-movie"* and find that you still continue to develop a cold or the flu, don't start feeling guilty. The guilt will only reinforce a *'belief'* that you deserved getting sick and it will wear down your immune system even more. Instead simply acknowledge, rather than denying, that for whatever reason, you now have *'a cold or the flu'* and that you are experiencing some unpleasant symptoms. Then ... get serious about creating and playing your *"mini-movie"* that will program your body to eliminate and neutralize quickly any of the unpleasant symptoms that you are experiencing.

By the way, besides reinforcing your *"mini-movie"*, follow all the traditional recommendations: such as, stay warm, drink plenty of liquids, don't over exert yourself, get plenty of rest -- we're sure you know them so use common sense and follow them. Lastly, if your symptoms do not improve or they become more severe, **SEE YOUR DOCTOR!** If you don't, ask yourself, *"What am I trying to prove?"* or *"What am I afraid of?"* If you're really sick, get some help!

Throughout both of our teaching careers, we have come across individuals who, for whatever reason, avoid seeking Medical help and advice from doctors and healthcare professionals like the plague (clever pun, don't you think?). It is not our place, desire or purpose to judge anyone for holding such *"personal beliefs."* However, having said that, we are not -- nor would we ever suggest to anyone that he/she should use the techniques provided in this book as a substitute for seeking 'Professional Medical Advice'. We say this because, even though we both truly believe that the human body has a phenomenal ability to heal itself, it does have its *"limits."*

And when the body reaches these limits, it may desperately require the skills and techniques of others who are Professionally Qualified to help it heal properly, and in some cases, help you to survive.

Maintaining Good Health is a Prerequisite to Living a *Life of Quality*:

As important as having these techniques may be to help you regain good health in your life, it is far more important not to jeopardize your good health in the first place.

Of course accidents do happen and genetics can predispose any person to develop a wide range of health problems and diseases. Having said that, it is important that you never leave your good health to *'chance"*. By choosing not to eat well or choosing to overeat, by choosing not to exercise or not to provide your body sufficient sleep and rest, by not choosing to eliminate *Behavioral Habits* that you know are detrimental to your health i.e. smoking, excessive drinking, indulging in dangerous drug taking, etc., you are subjecting your health and well-being to **chance**.

A quality life was meant to be **by choice ... not chance**. So if you continue to leave your health to *chance*, don't cry *'victim'* or *'why me?'* if you lose playing this *'game of chance'* with your health and your life.

Maintaining *'good health'* will never jeopardize or prevent you from *'enjoying'* life. Just the opposite. There is no way that you can strive to live *'A Life of Quality'* if you do not have your health -- it's simply a prerequisite for achieving the best that life has to offer. So promise yourself that you won't take that *chance* but rather make the *choice* to claim **"Good Health."**

Perhaps, just perhaps, you might want to begin affirming that you will be 90, 100 or more years old, and simply die of *"Natural Causes"* – which is definitely more attractive than dying much younger of *"Unnatural and Unnecessary Causes." ***We're just asking you to think about it ... just think...***

THE 4-STEP PROCESS:

This *4-Step Process for Problem Solving and Goal Setting* is a practical, simple and straightforward formula that can be applied at any time to help you solve problems and reach goals in your life. We suggest that you apply *4-Step Process* when programming the *Problem Solving* and *Goal Setting Techniques*. It will therefore be extremely beneficial for you to take a few moments and study the following chart to ensure that you clearly understand the 4-Steps and to ensure you receive maximum benefit from these Techniques.

PROBLEM-SOLVING & GOAL-SETTING

THE 4-STEP PROCESS

Problem →	Goal →	Solution →	Action
Step 1	*Step 2*	*Step 3*	*Step 4*
Define Problem	Create Goal	Choose Solution	Take Action
Current Reality	*Desired Reality*	*Decision Making*	*Making it happen*
What <u>IS</u>	How I want to <u>*BE*</u>	What I should <u>DO</u>	*Going for* <u>*IT*</u>
What's my problem?	What do I <u>*WANT*</u> instead?	What am I going to do about it?	Doing it!

Step 1- Problem Solving:

In this step, you need to become clear and concise as to what your problem *'really is'* and why you feel it is a problem. Do not make any assumptions about the *"problem"* until you have honestly determined that it is a problem in your life. In some cases, what other people may feel is a serious problem, is not actually a problem for you.

An example of this could be a situation where you are unemployed and unless you get a job ASAP, you will not be able to pay your rent, you will be evicted, your car will be repossessed, etc. Obviously this is something you don't want and therefore being *'Unemployed'* **'Is a Problem for You.'**

On the other hand, the same situation could exist in your life and it's not a problem. Yes, you are unemployed but you are extremely happy to be so. You are using your free time to write the book you've always wanted to write. As you had planned for this period of not working, you have sufficient money for the rent, electricity, etc. Therefore, in this situation, being *'Unemployed'* **'Is not a Problem for you'** regardless of what other people might say or feel. If it isn't a problem for you, don't waste your time *"trying to fix something that isn't broken."* If however, you feel your unemployment is a *'Problem'*, then proceed to **Step 2**.

Step 2-Goal-Setting:

Having decided that you do have a problem in **Step 1**, it is in this **Step 2** that you will shift your thinking from *"Problem Solving"* to *"Goal Setting."* It is in this **Step 2** that you will need to clarify precisely what you want and/or how you want things to be. In other words, you are defining your **Goal**.

Step 3-Solution:

Once you have determined what your goal will be, it will be here in **Step 3** where you will need to determine what you will need to do to achieve your **Goal.** And once you have done so, you will move to the next and last Step in the process.

Step 4 - Action:

In this Step, you will need to get off of your behind and actually follow through and do whatever was determined needed to be done in the **Step 3**.

This **Step 4** is usually the easiest of all the Steps as you already know precisely what you need to do. We have found, however, that this Step is often the one that most people resist doing. Even if all the hard work has been done in the previous Steps, some people, for whatever reason, put on the brakes, and procrastinate by finding endless excuses for not doing what they know they need to do. Even though they may only need to make one phone call, they don't do it. Perhaps it's because they are afraid. Afraid to get what they really want or afraid of the responsibilities that might go with it. Perhaps they are afraid of challenging some deep-seated *'Disempowering Belief'* they have about themselves or they are afraid of succeeding for some other reason. Regardless of the reason, they choose not to succeed.

As for you, we cannot stress enough the importance of following through on all of the **4 Steps**. And unless you do, your deepest desires which might be a mere *1 Step away* but they will never be realized in your life. If you choose not to take that final Step, we are not suggesting you should feel guilty or feel you have done anything wrong, you haven't. Taking steps to your success will always be your <u>choice</u>. So if you decide not to have what you really want in life, then in simple fairness, don't *'blame others'* or *'your circumstances'* because the truth will be that it was your *choice* and yours alone. Fair enough? Good!

The Problem-Solving and Goal-Setting Technique:

Whether you are solving a problem or striving to reach your goal, the programming procedure is essentially the same. The only difference is there are *2-Steps required for Problem-Solving* while there is only *1-Step required for the Goal-Setting*.

If you desire to *Solve a Problem*, begin with **Step1**, which will be to clarify the nature of the your problem. Once you have done so, you move to **Step 2**, where you will decide what you do want (or how you want things to be) instead.

If you desire to *Program a Goal*, begin with **Step 2**. The reason for this is that if you don't have a problem, there is no sense in imagining or creating one, is there?

The Technique:

Begin by *Centering* yourself. Don't take your *Centering* for granted. Be sure you are sufficiently relaxed both physically and mentally before you begin to '*Solve your Problems*' or '*Set your Goals*'. Once you feel you are *Centered*, you can begin your programming.

1. If you desire to use the *Problem Solving Technique*: **Start with Step 1 -- The Problem Phase**.

2. If you desire to use a Goal-Setting Technique: **Proceed directly to Step 2 -- The Goal Phase**.

Step 1 -- Problem Solving:

Bring to your *Mind* an image of the Problem you're concerned with and would like to solve. Then start thinking about your Problem. Determine why you feel it is a problem and what influence or impact it is having in your life? Do not rush this process. It is important that you honestly and fully *"Face the Problem"*, not avoid it.

Make mental note of any negative emotional reaction(s) or feelings you experience when you analyze the problem, such as: anger, stress, fear or any other feeling. Remember, it is these deep-seated reaction/feelings that have caused you to want to be free of this problem, so again, don't deny them. Remember, the objective of **Step 1** is to determine what the real problem is and why you desire to be free of it.

When you have done so, ask yourself *"Do I really want to be free of this problem in my life?"* If your answer is 'No', simply stop your programming as you have determined that you really don't have a

142

problem. However, if your answer is **'Yes'**, imagine, by any means you can, eliminating this problem, and all of its negative feelings, from your *Mind* and your life.

This can be done by imagining erasing the problem with an eraser or imagining that you are attaching that *'problem'* to a huge balloon, then imagine that balloon drifting away and taking your problem with it and far away from your life. Of course you can use any other means you can think of to imagine that problem is leaving your life ... forever. By using your *Mind* to imagine that a problem is leaving your life by a balloon (or by some other way), you are using *'images or pictures'* to communicate your desire to be free of this problem to your *Subconscious Mind*. Remember that *'images and pictures'* is how the *Subconscious* communicates. That is why when we dream they are in the form of *'images or pictures'*.

When you feel that your *'problem'* has been taken away, you will have in a sense, created a void within you. It will be at this time that you will need to move to **Step 2** in order to fill this void with what you do want instead, which is *your Goal.*

Step 2 -- Goal-Setting:

Create in your Mind an image of *'what you do want'*. When you create this image, you are creating your *Goal*. When you have done so, begin to modify this image of your *Goal* so that it precisely indicates what you want and/or how you would want things to be.

Do not -- limit yourself or restrict yourself to imagining your *Goal* based upon what you think is possible. Rather imagine exactly as how you truly *'want things to be'*. Any limitations or restrictions that you place on your *Goal* will actually be reflecting some fear you have of achieving it or your lack of belief that you could actually achieve it.

Always be as specific as possible -- include as many details as possible to precisely create the *Goal* that you truly desire. When you feel that the image you have created in your *Mind* is exactly what you want, say to yourself *'This is what I want'* ... *and this is what I will have .. and this is the truth'*, then take a deep breath and relax your thinking.

You can now finish this programming session if you so desire or you can begin programming to solve another *Problem* or to create another *Goal* that you may have.

What You Have Achieved by Programming Your Goal at Your Subconscious Level:

By going through this process, you have embedded or *planted* deeply within your *Subconscious* your precise *Goal*. What will be required in the future will be for you to water and nurture the seeds of that *Goal* which you have planted.

To nurture your Goal, *Center* yourself and begin reinforcing your embedded *Goal*. Now however, imagine in your *Mind* that you have already reached this goal. Make it as real as you can in order to create the feeling that you already have achieved your *Goal*. The reason for this is that your *Subconscious Mind* does not respond to the time-line of *Past -- Present -- Future*. The *Subconscious* always functions exclusively in the *Present*. By the way, that is why all of your dreams are experienced as happening in the *Present*, regardless of whether you are dreaming about the past, the present or the future.

Therefore it is very important to remember that when reinforcing your *Goal*, always imagine that you have already achieved it (Present). Imagine the feelings you would actually have knowing that you have successfully achieved your *Goal*. Perhaps for you it might be feelings of joy, happiness, pride, super confidence, etc., if so, then imagine as best as you can actually feeling that way. By doing so, you are transforming your desired future into your present reality and thereby reinforcing your success in achieving that goal. In other words, you are seeing (or imagining) yourself successful, and as they say, *"Seeing is Believing!"*

How Often Do You Need to Reinforce Your Goal?

Reinforce your *Goal* every time you think of it during the day. When you do *"think about it,"* always think about it as if it has already been achieved it in your life.

We strongly recommend that you reinforce your *Goal* at least once a day, for 21 days while you are Centered. This 21 day time period may initially seem to be a long time, but think about it, it is a mere 3 weeks. Three weeks that can make one of your dreams a reality and change your life forever.

Having said that, we are not saying that it will necessarily take a full 3 weeks to achieve your *Goal.* You might get it so fast that *"your head will spin* (or at least your Mind within it will)". What we are saying is that within 21 days of programming you most probably will have either received:

1.   A solution as to how you can obtain your Goal

2.   The Goal itself

If however, after 3 weeks you have not received *any indication* that you are making *any progress* towards achieving your Goal, we recommend that you start rethinking your *Goal.* Pay particular attention to the intensity of your desire and/or any beliefs that you might have that may be sabotaging the success of your programming.

Be ultra-sensitive to any thoughts that may come to *Mind* when you are thinking about or attempting to program your *Goal.* These thoughts can provide important insight as to what you may need to look at in greater detail before you proceed to reprogram your *Goal.*

In addition, always be willing to challenge yourself by asking yourself a few very fundamental questions:

In Regards to Your Beliefs & Desires –

1.   Do I really believe I should be asking to have this (morally, ethically, etc.)?

2.   Am I worthy and/or capable of achieving my Desired Goal?

3.   Why do I really, really want it?"

145

As you continue to program for your *Goal*, don't be surprised if new issues and concerns begin to surface. These issues and concerns are the result of you getting closer to achieving your *Goal*. They usually are indicating that some fine-tuning is required. Just confront each them as they arise and incorporate any new understanding and insight that you gain into your future programming of that *Goal*. In short, "*keep your programming up-to-date.*"

Example:

If during your initial 3 weeks of programming, you become aware of the fact that you will most probably need some special training or some course in order to obtain the type of work you desire, then adjust your *Goal* so that it incorporates this need for additional training.

A Few More Important Facts to Consider When Programming

Your Goals:

Avoid falling into the trap of thinking that the more you program, the better. Of course you need to reinforce your *Goal* but this reinforcement is meant to be an *Affirmation* of your success. If you begin to feel, "*Oh, I forgot to program this morning -- I better program twice this evening,*" you are not affirming your belief of succeeding but rather you are reinforcing your belief *that you might fail*.

When we suggest that you program your *Goal* daily, it is not meant to imply that if you miss a day, you will not achieve your *Goal*. The purpose of your "*daily programming*" is to simply reinforce your expectation and desire to achieve your *Goal*.

In regards to how you can increase your desire to achieve a *Goal*, we must ask you, "*Why would there be a need to increase your desire?*" If you discover that you really don't want something after all, then what is the issue? You were successful in eliminating that concern or desire from your life,

If you find yourself thinking that you "*should*" want something more than you do, ask yourself -- "*Why?*" "*Why should I want that?*" Remember,

146

even though others might think you should want something, if you don't feel any desire to get it, don't program for it. Besides, programming to have something, just because *'others think you should'*, seldom works, so don't set yourself up to fail. Besides, it will only convey to your *Subconscious* a sense of *"failure"*. You really didn't fail, did you? ... You simply never really wanted it in the first place. Don't play around with programming for something you really don't want. It'll be a waste of your precious time. Use your time to get what you want – not what others want.

That's it, my friend. It is now time to start doing rather than just reading about it. As you begin, remember that your future has not yet been determined -- it is waiting for you to create it.

You have great power to create the life you desire, so create one that you will enjoy living to its fullest. Create your future wisely as it will be your legacy. Your life is a reflection of who you are, so start creating a *Life of Quality* ... a life you will be proud of.

Very Important!

Now is the time to start listening to the 2nd MP3 Recording: *Embedding Techniques* which can be downloaded from our website, It is a *'Guided Relaxation'* which will strongly embed all of the Techniques provided in this book. We strongly urge you to listen to the Embedding Techniques recording at least 4 times to ensure that all of the techniques will be firming implanted in your Subconscious and available for you use and benefit.

... begin creating your future by choice – rather than leaving it to chance.

You deserve the best – settle for nothing less and start now claiming the Life you desire and do it NOW! We truly wish you a *Life of Health, Wealth and Happiness.*

Tom and Elena

So now ...

Get Centered,

Get Excited, Get Going ...

And Start Creating

The Future You Dream Of!

The Creed

For Living A Life Of Quality

I choose to live a life of quality. I choose to take charge of my life for my life has meaning and purpose. I am a powerful, responsible, determined, and successful person. I am a leader, as I demonstrate what I advocate to others. I have confidence in myself and knowing that nothing can stop me.

Quality Life Training

I am enthusiastic about my life and I love living! I truly care about people and the quality of their lives. I love myself and I choose to share myself with others. I am comfortable making commitments to myself and to others. I am thinking and feeling human being. My time is valuable and I use my time wisely.

I know I have and I will always have a choice. I choose to live out of a commitment and purpose. I choose to grow and expand in knowledge and understanding. I choose to be healthy, happy and prosperous. I choose to effortlessly float in the rhythm of life, knowing that the Universe is my playground.

Today I Claim My Freedom ...
I Am Free!

IMPORTANT INFORMATION REGARDING PRINTING THE CHARTS & WORKSHEETS:

The book has provided a variety of *Charts & Worksheet* that have supplemented the material in this book. All of the Charts & Worksheets can be easily printed.

The 21-Day Journal Sheet:

We strongly recommend that you make a serious effort to record details of your responses that you have while using *"The Relaxation Training Exercise"* and the various Techniques. We strongly suggest that the *21 Day Journal* worksheet be printed for convenience.

The Audio Recordings:

The audio MP3 recordings – *"The Relaxation Training Exercise"* & *"Embedding Techniques"* can be downloaded from the website provided with this book.

21 Day Journal

You may want to have a different sheet for each of your various techniques.
Keeping a record of your responses will help you refine and
improve the Techniques that you use.

DAY	TIME	COMMENTS
DAY 1		
DAY 2		
DAY 3		
DAY 4		
DAY 5		
DAY 6		
DAY 7		
DAY 8		
DAY 9		
DAY 10		
DAY 11		
DAY 12		
DAY 13		
DAY 14		
DAY 15		
DAY 16		
DAY 17		
DAY 18		
DAY 19		
DAY 20		
DAY 21		

An Invitation to Attend
The QLT Seminar

The information in this book is based upon an intensive **2-day** QLT *Seminar,* which is taught in both English and Spanish. The *QLT Seminar* includes numerous additional techniques and skills that have been designed to enhance every aspect of the person's life.

For more information regarding *The QLT Seminar* **or when it will be offered in your area, please contact:**

The QLT Seminar in English:
tmahas@qltseminars.com

The QLT Seminar in Spanish:
contacto@qualitylifetraining.com

Or Visit:
www.qltseminars.com

What Others Have Said About
The QLT Seminar

"Enlightening and exciting! I was re-awakened to life's potential and the joy of living. Simply the best days I spent"
Financial Consultant – Sydney, Australia

"The QLT Seminar was wonderful!! I can honestly say that from the first few hours of the seminar, I knew this Seminar would change my life for the better."
J.E. University Student - Barcelona, Spain

"The QLT course was illuminating in a supportive and non-threatening way. Personally I gained self-awareness, Professionally I gained promotions, Financially I gained heaps!"
N.D. - C.E.O. - Miami, USA

"The experience that I had in the seminar is something very special. Being able to work with one's feelings and emotions, allowed people to strengthen their Self Esteem and the human spirit."
C.R. Psychologists - Santiago, Chile

About the Authors:

Elena Sotomayor CHC, is the Director of the Center for Hypnotherapy in Santiago, Chile. Born in Santiago, Elena relocated to Sydney, Australia in the early 1970s. Initially she dedicated her life to raising her two daughters. However, within a few years she began teaching Personal Development. It wasn't until 2000 that she decided to expand her Seminar Business to the USA. After having done so, she then returned to her home country, Chile, where she established the Center for Hypnotherapy and where she continues to reside. She obtained her Clinical Hypnosis Certificate from the University of Miami. She's a current member of the American Board of Hypnotherapy (ABH). She has presented her programs in Chile, as well as in Australia, USA, Spain.

Tom Mahas BA,MA, is the Director of Quality Life Training Seminars (QLT Seminars) in Sydney, Australia. Born in Milwaukee, Wisconsin, USA, he has been involved in presenting training programs for over 30 years. Tom has degrees in Psychology and Sociology from the University of Wisconsin, USA, as well as a Master's Degree in Adult Education from the National College of Education, USA. He relocated to Sydney, Australia in 1983 where he is still resides. Tom continues to present his seminars to major health agencies & hospitals, numerous schools and school systems, government agencies and corporate businesses, such as, Coca-Cola, Pepsi Cola, Arthur Andersen, United Group Ltd, throughout Australia, USA and Europe.